TOOTHPICK HOLDERS:
China, Glass and Metal

Prepared by members of the
National Toothpick Holder Collector's Society

©1992 ANTIQUE PUBLICATIONS
Box 553
Marietta, Ohio 45750

ALL RIGHTS RESERVED

ISBN # PB 0-915410-88-5
ISBN # HB 0-915410-89-3

Affectionately dedicated to the late
William Heacock
our mentor and good friend

TABLE OF CONTENTS

Acknowledgements vii

About NTHCS viii

Publishers Intro ix

Introduction x

Collecting Today xi

Categories of Collectible Toothpick Holders xii

Insuring Your Collection xvi

Description of Pictured Items 1-511 1-16

Color Photos 17-60

Miscellaneous Items 61-64

Description of Pictured Items 512-1174 65-86

B/W Photos 87-124

Bibliography 125-130

Index 131-136

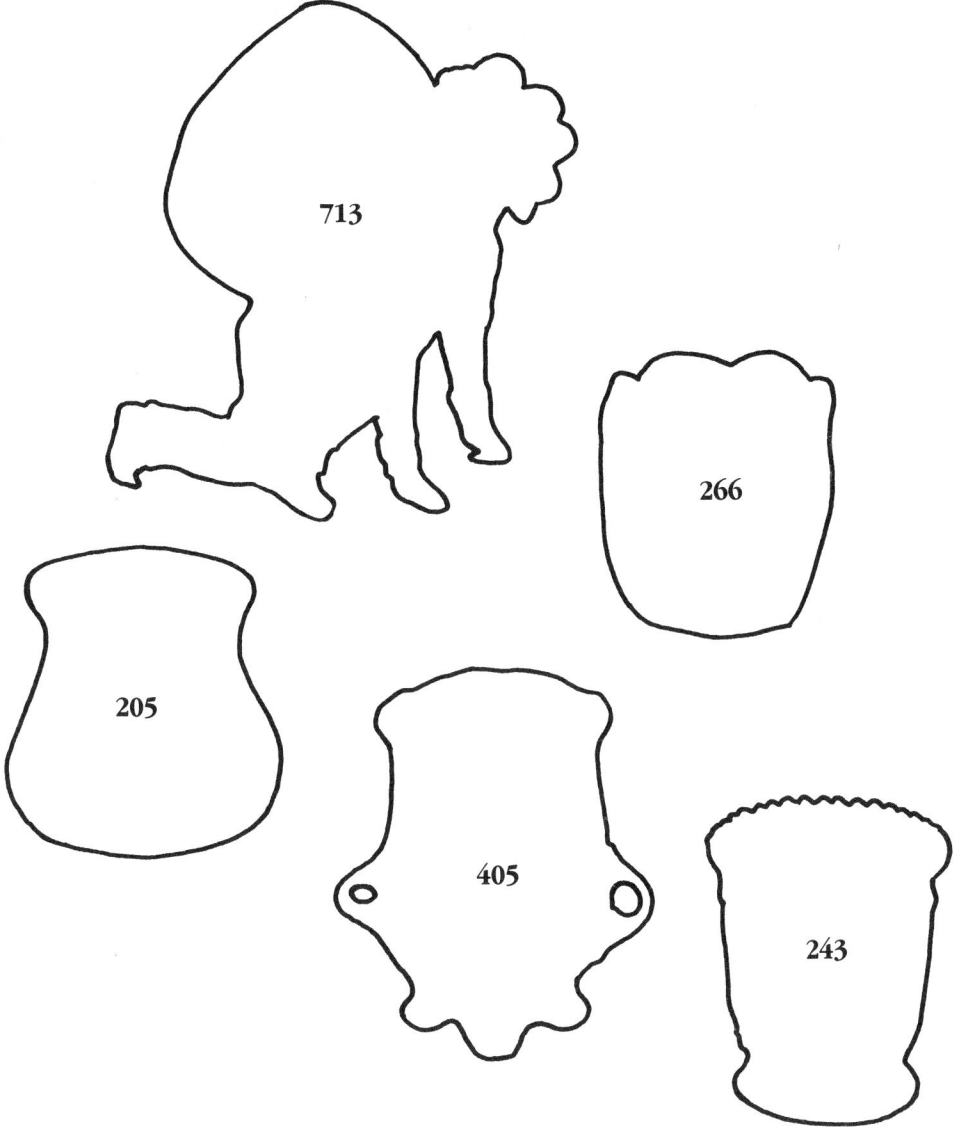

713. SILVERPLATE. Figural. Marked "MADE IN JAPAN". Indian with barrel on back.

266. DANDELION. Fostoria Glass Co. #1819, circa 1911. Clear and rare in ruby stain. Ref: H-1000 #635.

205. BLUE OPAQUE. New England Glass Co., circa 1886. Has ribbed optic effect. Color very rare. Ref: H-R/U #1053.

405. ROYAL BAYREUTH. Tapestry, Polar Bears. Unmarked. The shape and scene are typical. For shape see H-R/U #1415 and H-1000 #878.

243. LOCKET ON CHAIN. A.H. Heisey Co. #160, circa 1900-1902. Emerald green with gold. Also found in crystal, canary and an all-over ruby stain with gold trim. Ref: H-1000 #228.

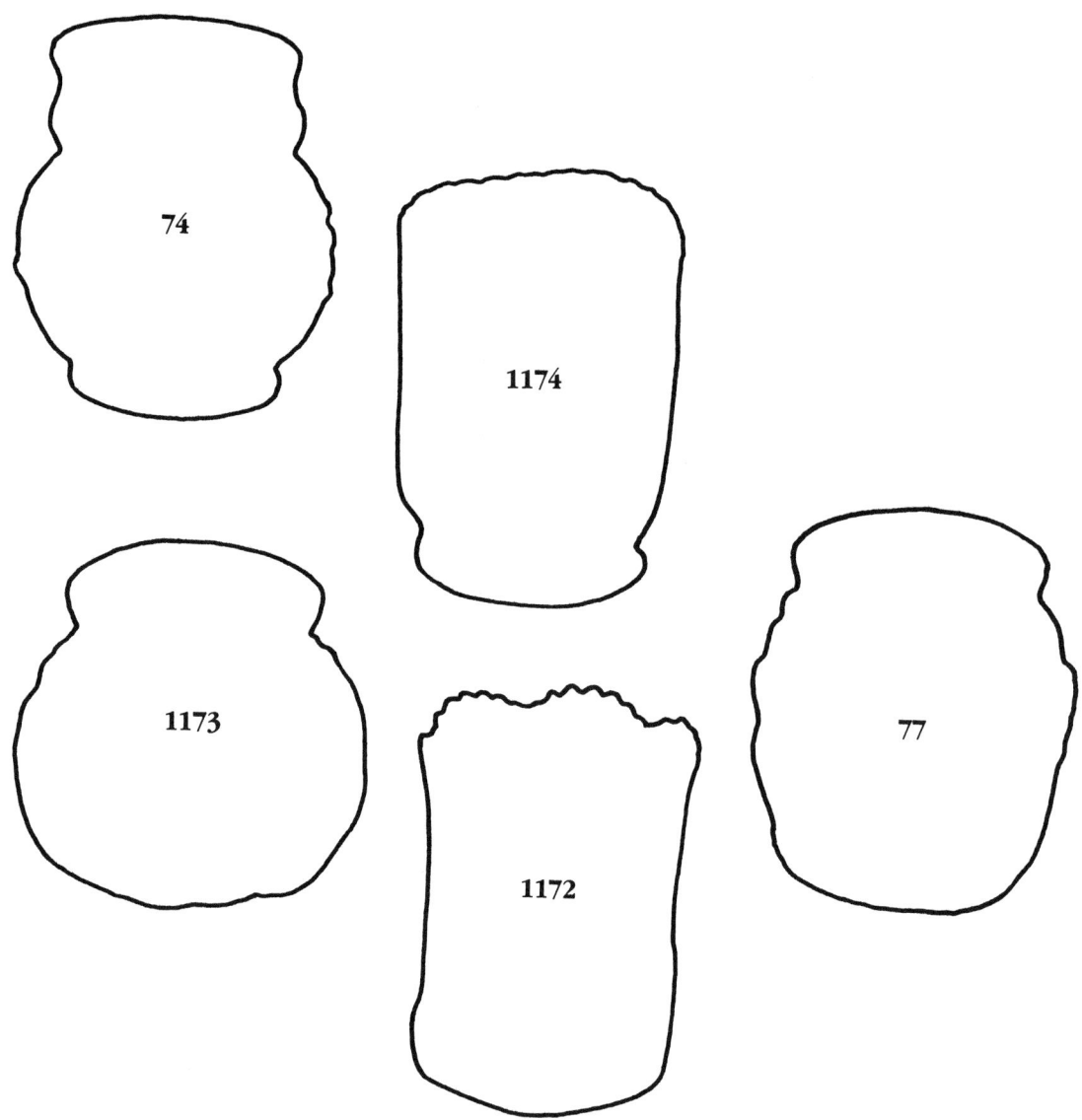

74. LEAF UMBRELLA. Northwood, circa 1889. Cranberry/white spatter with satin finish. Made in other Northwood colors. Ref: H-1 #'s 176-179 and HMW-NOR.

1174. WILLIAM R. HEACOCK COMMEMORATIVE TOOTHPICK HOLDER. Fenton Art Glass, 1991. Limited edition made for NTHCS 1991 convention. Burmese glass with photo decal of Heacock. Shape is like Madoline (aka Swinger in Ref: H-1000) pattern originally produced by Cooperative Flint Glass Co. about 1890. See also 259.

77. LEAF MOLD. Northwood, circa 1891. Yellow-green satin and tortoise shell spatter (cranberry, white, vaseline, and dark burgundy). Ref: H-1 #'s 169-175 and HMW-NOR.

1173. ROYAL IVY. Frosted rubina. The Northwood Glass Co., circa early 1890's. Made in many Northwood colors. Ref: H-1 #262-266; HMW-NOR.

1172. BUTTON ARCHES. Ruby stain, souvenired. Duncan Miller Glass Co., Washington, Pa., circa 1914. Pattern introduced in 1885 by George Duncan Co. and is still produced by other companies. Ref: H-1 #42.

ACKNOWLEDGEMENTS

Because there are so many people who have contributed to this reference and whom we want to acknowledge, it is difficult to know where to begin the "Thank You's." Let's start at the beginning and express our sincere gratitude to:

AL MILLS . . . who transformed an NTHCS dream into a viable project.

RON BAKER . . . who served as Chairman and was actively involved in flushing out many rare and unusual toothpick holders, organizing and directing the photography session and securing the participation of many members.

LEIGHTON FOSSEY . . . who oversaw the development of this project, provided legal counsel, and gave continuity and direction throughout the project.

COMMITTEE MEMBERS . . . who, among other things, were responsible for gathering, selecting, and organizing items for photography; providing expertise in identifying and describing the toothpick holders; and reviewing captions in their areas of expertise.

    HELEN BOYD   BOB McNAMARA
    BOB DAVIS   KAY MILLER
    GLENN HAVERFIELD   VIVIAN MUMFORD
    TOM JIAMACHELLO

HARRY WARE . . . who spent literally weeks researching and verifying information, writing text and compiling the Bibliography, with the able assistance of his wife, NANCY, who did all of the data entry and rewrites without complaint.

JUDY KNAUER . . . who assisted with the writing and did the final edit.

JIM MEASELL . . . who patiently and willingly guided us through the publication process, generously sharing his knowledge of glass.

DEANA WYNN . . . whose patience and skill resulted in the outstanding color plates and photographs included herein.

DAVE RICHARDSON . . . who encouraged this undertaking, and supported it by providing the personnel to guide us.

And last, but most certainly not least, all the NTHCS members who loaned their prized possessions for inclusion in this reference:

Ron and June Arnison; Iva Bader; C. Ron Baker; Fred Basden; Greg and Connie Boyd; Helen and Lee Boyd; Wilfred Cohen; John and Wilma Conner; Bob Davis; Louise Dinwiddie; Sue Durbin; Red and Betty Edwards; Dick and Eileen Flaks; Leighton and June Fossey; Bernadine Hagan; Bill and Liz Hartman; Glen and Vera Haverfield; Ralph and Marguerite Higdon, Wally and Pat Hipshear; Keith and Lorraine Holt; Sarah Jenkins; Albert and Marguerite Jiamachello; Tom Jimachello; Ron and Betty Jordan; Charlene Kelbley; Eleanor Kerr; Judy Knauer; Tom and Betty Kullman; Gene and Diana Kunzler; Charles and Marilyn Lockwood; Robert and Mona MacDonald; Jim and Betty Maquire; Joe and Arlene Makarewicz; Carol Malan; Marion and Robert McArthur; Maurine McBroom; Leroy McDiarmid; Phil and Edna McLain; Mary Melloh; Kathryn Miller; Russ and Vivian Mumford; Russ and Betty Musgrove; Lorene Otto; Tom and Dorothy Passamonte; Fred and Mary Petersen; Ruth Quinn; Fred and Isabel Raether; Carlene Rouse; Marvin and Ruby Rutishauser; Bruce and Toby Shugart; Leo and Pauline Soderholm; Patricia Stelter; Carol Trego; Rich and Mary Lou Trunkey; and Harry and Nancy Ware.

If anyone has inadvertently been omitted from this recognition, we are truly sorry. So many people played an important role in bringing this book to fruition, and we want to acknowledge our appreciation to each and every one.

-NTHCS Book Committee

THE NATIONAL TOOTHPICK HOLDER COLLECTOR'S SOCIETY

Founded in 1973, the National Toothpick Holder Collector's Society (NTHCS) numbers over 600 members. While the specific specialties of the members vary, all enjoy the common bond of collecting toothpick holders.

The monthly *Toothpick Bulletin*, the official publication of NTHCS, offers a variety of articles that include information on specific patterns or manufacturers, reproductions, newly discovered information on toothpick holders, previously undocumented toothpick holders, questions and answers from members, and notification of related events. Of a less formal nature, it also includes "Lucky Finds" and interesting stories submitted by members, as well as ads for buying and/or selling toothpick holders.

The year 1976 was a banner year for NTHCS. We held our first national convention and introduced our first exclusive toothpick holder. Both events were so well received that they have been repeated annually.

The annual convention is held in a different location each year and features several activities so popular with members that they have become traditions. Each year, time is devoted to touring points of interest near the host city, attending educational seminars, an Identification Clinic, a toothpick holder auction, a toothpick holder raffle and, on the last day, a public Toothpick Holder Show featuring competitive displays.

NTHCS is a unique organization, dedicated to enhancing the enjoyment of collecting toothpick holders as a hobby. We strive to learn more about these little gems, their origins and their history.

For a complimentary copy of the *Toothpick Bulletin*, write to:

Judy Knauer, Founder and Editor
NATIONAL TOOTHPICK HOLDER COLLECTORS SOCIETY
1224 Spring Valley Lane
West Chester, PA 19380

PUBLISHER'S INTRODUCTION

For me, it all began in the summer of 1974, when a tall, skinny, red-headed "kid" came to see my father about a job of printing. In the years since this happened, I have recalled and chuckled many times over the letter my dad wrote to me describing this incident.

"Well, son, I just have to take a couple of minutes to tell you about this kid that came to see me today. I was having one of my typical Mondays when the girl out front comes in to announce that there's a young man from Michigan here to see me about printing a book on toothpicks. I immediately thought to myself here's one of these people we get from time to time who live in a dream world and who have some crazy idea that they think is going to make them a million dollars. Imagine, Dave, a book about toothpicks! Some are round and some are flat; some are wooden and some are plastic. What more can you say about toothpicks and who'd be interested anyway?

"It wasn't very long after he came into my office that I realized that the book he wanted us to print wasn't about toothpicks but about toothpick **holders**! I guess everybody in the glass world calls them 'toothpicks' for short. I told him quite frankly that the idea stank! 'No way am I going to print a book like that.' 'Why not?' he wanted to know. And I told him -'Because every time somebody has a great idea that doesn't work, the printer gets left holding the bag for the cost of the book.' That's when he offered to sell his collection to pay for the book if it was a bad idea. I was impressed with his attitude - he thought it was a good idea and nothing I could do would shake him from that position. Well, Dave, I figured we're in the printing business, if this kid wants to waste his money on doing a book that only his grandmother will buy, who am I to stop him?"

My father is great at making predictions. (He's the one who said in 1960 that America wasn't ready to elect a Catholic President!) Even though he was sure the idea was bad, we printed that book anyway. It was a year and a half later, in 1975, when I got home from the service that I finally got to meet this "kid" and judge for myself the literary value and marketability of his book. The book was called *The Encyclopedia of Victorian Colored Pattern Glass, Book 1, Toothpick Holders from A to Z*, and this "kid," I discovered much to my surprise, was really a young man about my own age and his name was Bill Heacock.

From that first book came a series of books on Victorian pattern glass and much success, and from that meeting came a thirteen-year friendship between Bill and me. Among the many books he published during that time were two more books on toothpick holders (*1000 Toothpick Holders: A Collector's Guide* and *Rare and Unlisted Toothpick Holders*). In 1976 Bill helped found the National Toothpick Holder Collectors Society, and it was at their tenth anniversary convention in 1986, after his terminal illness was well advanced, that he made his last public appearance to say good-bye to his friends.

At the NTHCS convention in 1989, a year after Bill's death, I was invited to speak and was asked by the club what could be done to memorialize our mutual friend. My prompt answer was that Bill could best be remembered by the publishing of another book on toothpicks. He had often told me that ". . . one day we will have to do a book on the other toothpicks . . ." meaning ones that were not shown in any of his three books. I urged NTHCS members to bring together as many of "the other toothpicks" as they could find and together we would publish another book. The volume you are now reading is the result of that effort.

To all of the people who have devoted so much time and effort into bringing this book into being, for all current collectors of TPs who will benefit from this book, for all future collectors of TPs who will learn from this research, I say "thank you."

And I hope that this book helps keep alive the memory of a very special friend, Bill Heacock.

David E. Richardson, Publisher
June 1, 1993

INTRODUCTION

This book is the result of the efforts of many members of the National Toothpick Holder Collector's Society (NTHCS). After a year of planning and gathering information, the Book Committee scheduled a photo session to coincide with the annual convention held in Marietta, Ohio, in August, 1991. Members attending were asked to bring any previously undocumented toothpick holders with them.

And bring toothpick holders they did! Can you picture thousands of these little items arranged in two small hotel rooms? Combine that with the challenge of sorting and selecting among similar items to be included in a single photo, taking them to and from the photography studio, and not losing the description or the owner's identity in the process. Quite an undertaking! In total, almost 1200 toothpick holders were photographed.

While our primary objective was to picture previously undocumented items, we have also included some toothpick holders shown for the first time in rare or unusual colors or decorations. Since we are presenting so many items not pictured in other references, there is often little background information available. Every effort has been made to minimize unfounded speculation, and, as you are aware, the experts do not always agree.

A number of the items included in this reference are open to discussion as to their original utilitarian purpose. Some we know were not produced as toothpick holders, but are included here as they are frequently valued additions to collections as representative of a particular type of glass, the work of a specific artist, or an historical era. Original catalogs show us that a number of items were produced for multiple purposes, such as "toothpick or match holder" or "toothpick or whiskey (shot) glass." Still others were listed simply as "novelty" items. Art glass items were primarily intended for decorative purposes, and many pieces were made with no particular function in mind. Most collectors, however, are proud to include this category in their collection even though some items would not function well as toothpick holders.

Every effort has been made to provide accurate, valid information on each item pictured. Knowledgeable members specializing in the various collectible categories have reviewed the captions to help achieve this goal. We did not report information based on hearsay or tales told to the buyer when the toothpick holder was purchased. Speculation as to age and origin was avoided unless there was some strong basis for stating "probably." Where we were less certain, but had reason to believe an attribution was likely, we used the term "possibly." Many references are cited in the text, and many more are included in the bibliography for those interested in investigating beyond what is presented here. Hopefully, further research and new information that this reference is likely to generate will provide us with more definitive attributions as to age and origin.

We welcome your feedback on this reference and any additional information you may be able to provide. Research on antiques and collectibles is a dynamic field, and there will always be more to learn. As active collectors, we look forward to this pursuit with enthusiasm!

COLLECTING TODAY

Collecting has never been as popular as it is today. You name it, and there is someone collecting it. In fact, there is a good chance you will find an organization of collectors devoted to the item.

Several interesting phenomena accompanying this collecting craze are worth noting. Even items of fairly recent vintage are highly sought after. Check the prices for metal lunch boxes your children carried to school or on Star Wars memorabilia. Kitchenwares of the '50s and '60s are highly sought after by the younger generation as they establish their own households. Some items are even produced as "collectibles" and qualify for that category immediately upon issue.

Notice also the ages of collectors. People in all age categories flock to the flea markets, auctions, antique malls and shows. If you check out the booths and shops which carry sports cards, you'll find the lower end of the age range is very young indeed. And these youngsters are very knowledgeable in their fields!

For every collectible item, there is at least one reference book published. This has probably been a factor in encouraging collecting as a hobby, and it has probably contributed to bringing collectors with similar interests together. The references not only provide information on our collectibles, but they facilitate communications among collectors.

Along with this rapidly escalating collecting craze, shops now frequently advertise "antiques and collectibles," since buyers are not necessarily looking for items from many years ago. A word of caution—this also gives dealers license to carry new and reproduced items. Which brings us to the next obvious trend—reproductions.

Few, if any, collectibles are free from reproductions. Long a thorn in the collector's side, reproduction items make collecting even more challenging, given the recent avalanche of reproductions. The old adages "Know your dealer" and "If it seems too good to be true, it probably is," still apply. Know your collectible, and know it well.

Reproductions plague the "toothpick" market as much as any other. New china decorated with decals bear fake R. S. Prussia marks. Many, many glass patterns have been reproduced. Art glass imported from European countries closely resembles old art glass toothpicks. In addition, small studio shops in the United States are currently producing high quality art glass. These are lovely representations of today's art glass and are not reproductions, but they can cause confusion for a novice collector or dealer. Occasionally, an organization or a manufacturer will "reissue" a toothpick holder in an original mold. While technically not a "reproduction," these items can be misleading if they do not carry a manufacturer's mark or a sponsor's name or logo.

The fascination of collecting toothpick holders can be attributed to several factors—their beauty; the endless variety; the opportunity to specialize within the category; and their small size—are reasons frequently given. Once a part of every table setting, the toothpick holders (commonly referred to as "toothpicks") from the late Victorian Era are now relatively difficult to find. Because of the scarcity and demand, prices have escalated. Items that could be found for a couple of dollars 10 or 15 years ago will carry price tags of $20 to $150 today.

Being a collector today means being an informed collector. We all make a few mistakes as we seek out our special treasures, but staying current will minimize the disappointments that we experience. Again, the old advice still applies and is worth repeating. Know your dealer. Know your collectible. Don't spend more than the item is worth to you. If it sounds too good to be true, it probably is.

Happy Collecting! May you have many wonderful "Lucky Finds"!!

CATEGORIES OF COLLECTIBLE TOOTHPICK HOLDERS

One reason for the popularity of collecting toothpick holders is the wide variety of options available to collectors. You may choose to be a generalist and collect any and all toothpick holders, or you can specialize in particular categories. For this same reason, toothpicks are frequently found in other specialized collections. Art glass is a good example. There are a number of art glass toothpick holders highly sought after by those who collect art glass in general, toothpick holders, heat sensitive glass, or New England glass.

Individuals sometimes limit their collections to those toothpicks that are three-handled, made by a specific company, hand painted china, advertisements for a particular attraction or state, ruby stained, metal, named after a state, a specific color, or any number of other qualifiers. These make a beautiful and interesting collection, while allowing the collector the opportunity to express individual tastes and preferences. Let's take a closer look at some of the general categories available to collectors.

Pressed and Pattern Glass

This is probably the most popular category. That is easily explained by the fact that there are many glass toothpick holders available and much has been published in this area. Heacock's three books on toothpick holders, his other glass publications and those of other authors provide the collector with sources of valuable information about the glass they collect. The information in this book is intended to supplement that which was previously published by Heacock. Included within the pressed and pattern glass category are items that matched a complete set of tableware, unique pressed patterns, blown pieces, clear items, colored items, decorated glass and opalescent glass. It is open to discussion as to whether some of the more artistic colored glass items should be included in this category or with art glass. Authorities do not always agree on the definition of art glass.

Reproductions are a major concern in collecting glass. Many patterns have been reproduced in a wide variety of colors over the years. In addition, several contemporary glass makers are currently making toothpick holders that are not reproductions of old patterns, but that may be easily confused with old glass. Study the available publications. Being informed can save dollars and help you avoid the unhappy feeling of being "taken."

Condition is a prime concern when purchasing glass. A little wear is to be expected on an item that was in use for so many years, but choice pieces will be in "mint" condition. Chips, flakes and cracks will greatly devalue glassware. As a general rule, colored items are more desirable and, therefore, more expensive than clear glass.

Another factor that affects price is collectibility—supply and demand. A clear Kings Crown is fairly common and might sell for $15, while a clear Queen Anne by Heisey is scarce and will command several hundred dollars. Again, follow the "rule of thumb" when considering price. Ask yourself if it is worth that much to you.

Metal

Most metal toothpick holders are from the Victorian Era and are silverplated. A few are pot metal, sterling or other metals. The most highly prized and, therefore, most expensive are the Victorian figurals. Many of the silverplated items have a manufacturer's mark on the bottom, giving collectors a clue as to age. The books by Rainwater (see Bibliography) are good sources for mark identification.

Aluminum is more recent, but quite a variety of toothpick holders may be found in this metal. Considerably less expensive than the silverplate, this is one category that is found in the lower price ranges. Being softer, these toothpicks were highly subject to damage. Because of their light weight, they are frequently found with a weighted base. Often, you will find a small aluminum tray that holds the toothpick holder and matching salt and pepper shakers.

Condition is again a prime consideration. While less fragile than glass, the metal items are subject to dents, rim distortion and, in the case of figurals, pieces being missing or distorted.

Opinions differ on the importance of the quality of the plating. If the items were used, much of the silver may be worn off. Some owners choose to have the items replated to restore the original shiny finish.

Reproductions are less of an issue in this field. One does need to look out for items that resemble toothpick holders, but were originally intended as match or cigarette holders. Figural napkin rings have enjoyed strong collector interest for many years. This and the fact that those collectors tend to also include the toothpick holders have escalated prices on these items.

Porcelain and China

Although many china toothpick holders are available, there is very little information on them. There are many excellent references on china, but few toothpick holders are pictured or documented. It may be difficult to determine if an item is really a toothpick holder or something else, such as a small vase. Many china items were sold as "novelties" with no specific utilitarian purpose in mind. Only a few china pieces were marked by the manufacturer or, in the case of the hand painted ones, signed by the artist.

These are highly subject to chips and cracks and should be examined carefully for damage. Reproductions are less prevalent here than in glassware, but fake marks (decals) have been found on contemporary china. Available items range from fairly coarse pottery to fine, delicate china. Value is determined by condition, artistry (fine quality hand painted scenes vs. decal work, shape, etc.), quality of the china and, to a large extent, if it is a known "name." Some of the more highly collectible china is discussed below.

R. S. Prussia is known for its interesting shapes, delicate handles and fine artistry. Some, but not all, pieces are marked. The "red mark" (red print with green lettering) is most highly prized. Pieces marked "R. S. Germany" (or "R. S. Poland" or "R. S. Tillowitz") are from the same area and were produced by the same family of manufacturers. Items marked "Hand Painted" were generally decorated at the factory. Those that do not carry that mark, but are signed by an artist, were generally decorated after they left the factory. Since the toothpick holders are generally not easily mistaken for anything else and were often part of a table set, the excellent references that are available on this china are good sources of information as to patterns, dates and marks.

Royal Bayreuth is another highly collectible kind of china toothpick holder. These items are always scarce, and many are rare. Known for their variety of unusual shapes and interesting scenes, these items may be decorated with decals or hand painted.

This book plus Heacock's *Rare and Unlisted Toothpick Holders* will provide the reader with a wide variety of the shapes and patterns. Royal Bayreuth is known for the Tapestry finish applied to some items and for several series of designs: Sunbonnet Babies, Snow Babies, Sand Babies, Dutch Children, and Nursery Rhymes. Figural toothpick holders are another popular Royal Bayreuth collectible—Elkhead, Horsehead, Lamplighter, Rose, Devil and Card—to name a few. They also produced a number of items decorated with animals, Cavaliers, and portraits. *Royal Bayreuth*

China by Virginia and George Salley is frequently cited as a popular reference with collectors. Fortunately, most Royal Bayreuth items are marked.

Nippon is becoming increasingly popular as a collectible. Exported from Japan from 1891 to 1921, Nippon varies widely in the quality of the china as well as the decoration. Prices generally relate to the excellence of the hand decoration and scarcity. The word "Nippon" means Japan, and does not refer to a specific manufacturer. Nippon was made by many factories and is found with many different marks. Several excellent references on Nippon give detailed information on the various marks. Wares exported after 1921 are generally marked "Japan" or "Made in Japan."

Much of the decoration on Nippon pieces is hand painted. Those with the greatest amount of detail and artistry are highly sought after today. Toothpick holders were made in many shapes, but here again, some are easily confused with the components of smoking sets or dresser sets. As a general rule, toothpick holders are not likely to have straight sides or a flat, smooth top rim.

Doulton and *Royal Doulton* wares were produced by the Doulton Company starting in 1815. Many of the items now collected as toothpick holders were originally intended as novelties or cabinet pieces. The most collectible are the following series: Dickensware (1911-1940's), Robin Hood (1911-1940's), Nursery Rhymes (1930-present), and Bunnykins (1933-present). Again, there are good reference books devoted to Doulton.

Goss is another highly collectible ware. They were the most popular of a number of manufacturers producing so-called "crested" pieces, souvenir items so named because they often bore the crests of heraldry. These items were made in England beginning about 1880. Goss items are known in many shapes, some representing monuments, light houses, crosses, fonts, kettles, cottages, etc. Although they were not originally produced as toothpick holders, they are included here since many are toothpick size and are included in toothpick holder collections. The company and its trademarks are now owned by Ridegway Potteries Ltd.

Art Glass

Art Glass items are highly collectible for several obvious reasons. They represent some of the most beautiful work in the glass industry. In addition, the hand work required and the complex processing of the glass means that production of these items was more limited. There are a number of types of art glass—Burmese, Cameo, Agata, Peachblow—and several processes are generally involved in their making. Many of them are "heat sensitive" glass, meaning that the coloration changes when the item or portions of the item were reheated. Others involve delicate hand finishing processes to give them a special luster or texture. Some involve multiple steps in the blowing to produce an optic effect in the body of the glass. Much old art glass was not signed and paper labels that may have been applied are long gone. Well-known names include Mt. Washington, Webb, Tiffany, Loetz, Moser, Durand and Gallé and certainly a number of others. Much of this glass was made in the United States, England, and countries on the European continent.

Several challenges face today's art glass collector. First of all, prices are considerably higher than for most other glass forms. Also, reproductions have plagued the market. Contemporary art glass can also cause confusion when trying to attribute the age and manufacturer. Fortunately, many contemporary glass artists are signing their items. Identifying the manufacturer can be a challenge, too, since glassmakers moved from one location to another, taking their knowledge and skills with them. And, of course, when a type of glassware achieved popularity, other manufacturers tried to copy what was successful.

Art glass has been well covered in the literature. A number of excellent references provide information on the process as well as the origins of much of this glassware.

Cut Glass

Cut glass may be the remaining "frontier" for toothpick holder collectors. While there are a lot of excellent references on cut glass, very little mention is given to toothpick holders. Collectors of cut glass seem to prefer the larger, more elaborate items. Here again, since little is known about cut glass toothpick holders, collectors seem to be less excited about them.

Important considerations when buying cut glass include condition, color, weight and complexity of cut. The more valuable items will be heavy for their size, sparkling clear, and the cut design will be deep and cover a large portion of the body of the item. Signatures and marks are also important factors. Most pieces are unsigned, and those that are can be difficult to detect. A Hawkes, Libbey, Waterford, Dorflinger or Clark mark, for example, would greatly increase the value of the item. When considering shapes, the unusual are more desirable-pedestals, pedestals with ball in the stem, peg legs, footed, square or triangular blanks. Newer cut glass may be characterized by thinner, lighter weight blanks, more shallow cutting, and less intricate designs that cover less of the body of the item.

Reproductions are not yet an issue in this area, but the alert collector needs to be aware of fake signatures or marks. Many lead crystal items made today stand on their own and are not duplicates of older cut glass toothpick holders.

Cracked cut glass loses its value, but some chips and nicks can be polished out, restoring the item to nearly new condition. When these repairs are not obvious, they do not necessarily affect the value of the item. Collectors need to be aware of items similar in size and shape that may be small mustard jars, cut off salt shakers or small vases. Check the dimensions carefully and also check the position of the design. If the design is too near the top, the item may have been ground down.

NTHCS member Bob Davis has been researching cut glass toothpick holders and has provided much of the information for those pictured in this book. Where names of patterns were not previously known, he has created names. These will be changed if the original manufacturer's name becomes known.

Contemporary Studio or Art Glass

This category has become very popular in this country in recent years. A wide variety of very beautiful, fine quality art glass has been produced. Terry Crider has made a number of lovely toothpick holders, and others such as Dominic Labino, Charles Lotton and Joel Bloomberg produce a wide variety of items including some small items that may be collected as toothpick holders. Most of these artists sign their work.

There are several glass factories in this country still producing toothpick holders, and these are quite collectible for those who enjoy the new glass. Lovely for both their design and their color, they are included in many collections. Many of these companies now mark their glass so it will not be confused with the old.

Whatever you choose to collect, we hope you will find this reference book informative and enjoyable.

INSURING YOUR COLLECTION

How do I protect my collection from loss? Is there anything I can do?

The best answer to questions involving insuring a collection is to contact the insurance agent who handles your homeowner's or renter's coverage. If your collection is relatively small, a standard policy may cover it; some policies, however, specifically exclude collections. If covered, you may be required to provide proof of ownership. In some cases, an appraisal may be required. Policies vary from state to state, and certainly among different insurance companies, so be sure you are able to meet the criteria established by your specific company.

For larger collections or those where the value is high, special coverage may be required. In some cases, a "fine arts rider" is added to your policy. Again, check with your insurance agent. Ask about ways to insure your items, what type of losses are covered and what documentation is needed for proof of ownership.

The insurance company may ask you to inventory your collection. In some cases, they may even allow you to indicate value if you can demonstrate that it is based on current price guides or other documentation they are willing to accept. If you are taking inventory or appraising your own collection, remember to use replacement cost as opposed to what you paid for the item. The insurance company's claims resolution responsibility is to "restore you to your pre-loss status" as opposed to reimbursing you for your cash outlay. Again, work with your agent to be sure that what you are doing is acceptable.

The insurance company frequently will require a professional appraisal of your collection. This can be difficult for several reasons. First, a general appraiser is not likely to be knowledgeable in such a specialized field. Therefore, your best appraiser is someone active in your field of specialization. Finding someone able and willing can be a challenge. Some of those best qualified are not likely to be certified appraisers. Again, work with your agent. Professional ethics dictate that the appraiser will not buy items that they are appraising because this creates a conflict of interest. Be sure to state up front that this appraisal is for insurance purposes.

If you hire a professional appraiser, be sure to discuss the fee or charges in advance. Many charge a percentage of the total value of the appraised items. Others may charge by the hour or simply require a flat fee. Discuss what documentation the appaiser will provide for you. Will it be an itemized listing with individual prices for each item? Will it be a general listing with a total value for the collection? Know how much you are paying and what you are paying for.

Only you can determine if it is important for you to have your collection insured. Discuss it with your insurance agent so you can make an informed decision. Consider your risks, and be sure you understand exactly what kinds of losses are covered, the costs involved and the required documentation to establish proof of ownership.

1. ART GLASS, ruffled holder in brass base. Firey translucence. Possibly European, probably circa 1890's. Hand painted floral decoration.

2. DIAMOND POINT holder marked Pairpoint. Cigarette holder from the "Fine Arts" line, circa 1920's-1930's.

3. DAISY AND BUTTON holder by Duncan or Bryce, blue in silverplate frame marked Rogers and Bros. Circa 1890's. Ref: H-1 #89 and #90.

4. AMBERINA, square top, straight sides, Diamond Quilt holder by New England Glass/W.L. Libbey in silverplate frame marked James W. Tufts. Circa 1885-1895.

5. HAND PAINTED GLASS holder suspended by silverplate frame which is marked "AURORA S.P. MFG. CO. QUADRUPLE PLATE, WARRANTED, 0339".

6. BURMESE, hexagon top, glossy finish, decorated holder in silverplate frame marked "MERIDEN QUAD-RUPLEPLATE. Holder attributed to Thomas Webb and Sons, circa 1890's. Ref: H-1000, #80, updated H-R/U, p. 6.

7. INVERTED THUMBPRINT, BLUINA holder in silverplate frame marked "AURORA S.P. MFG. CO. QUADRUPLE PLATE, WARRANTED, A 347". Circa 1890. Ref: H-1000 #147 for shape and decor.

8. INVERTED THUMBPRINT, AMBERINA holder with ruffled top, Mt. Washington. Silverplate frame marked "AURORA S.P. MFG. CO. QUADRUPLE PLATE, WARRANTED, #338". Ref: H-R/U #1098.

9. BURMESE, Diamond Quilt, square top holder in silverplate frame marked "FORBES SILVER CO. QUADRUPLE". Circa 1890. Probably Thomas Webb & Sons.

10. BURMESE, tri-cornered holder in silverplate frame marked "J.A. BABCOCK & CO. QUADRUPLE PLATE", a company that went out of business in 1894. Holder is attributed to Mt. Washington Glass Co. Ref: H-1000 #47.

11. QUEEN MARY, probably Webb, in silverplate frame by James W. Tufts. Circa 1893. Ref: H-R/U #1075 and reported catalog listing.

12. CORALENE, Diamond Quilt, bulb base, flared top holder in silverplate frame marked "AURORA SILVERPLATE CO." Glass attributed is probably Mt. Washington. Circa 1890's.

13. ART GLASS, FLOWER FORM holder, in frame marked "EPNS" (Electro Plate Nickel Silver). English free form blown glass. Ref: H-1000 #528.

14. CAMEO GLASS with metal bands. Markings on bands appear to be "QUE" and "DE ROSSE" in a circular logo. Probably European, and possibly Daum Nancy.

15. PEACHBLOW, straight sides, square top. Mt. Washington Glass Co. Circa 1886. Decorations like H-R/U #1049 and color at base is bluish.

16. PEACHBLOW, bulb base, square top. Mt. Washington. Circa 1888.

17. BURMESE, two lobe holder, could be Mt. Washington or Thomas Webb & Sons, circa 1888, in silverplate frame marked "WM. ROGERS AND SON".

18. BURMESE, bulbous, footed with ruffled rim. Thomas Webb & Sons (England). Circa 1890.

19. BURMESE, hexagon top. Thomas Webb & Sons (England). Circa 1890. Ref: H-1000 #80.

20. BURMESE, square top, straight sides, Diamond Quilt. Mt. Washington, circa 1888.

21. BURMESE, square top, straight sides. Mt. Washington, circa 1880. Not Diamond Quilt as above. Ref: H-1000 #28.

22. BURMESE, round base, straight sides, ruffled (piecrust) rim. Mt. Washington Glass Co. based on decoration. Circa 1888.

23. BURMESE, bulb base, square top, Diamond Quilt. Mt. Washington Glass Co. Circa 1888.

24. BURMESE, glossy, bulb base, square top, Diamond Quilt. Mt. Washington Glass Co. Circa 1887.

25. BURMESE, bulb base, square top. Mt. Washington Glass Co. Circa 1887.

26. BURMESE, glossy, bulb base, square top, Diamond Quilt. Mt. Washington Glass Co. Circa 1887.

27. BURMESE, tri-corner, Diamond Quilt. Mt. Washington Glass Co. Circa 1888. Ref: H-1000 #4.

28. SIMULATED BURMESE, urn shape. Mt. Washington Glass Co. Circa 1890. Shading is a stain.

29. BURMESE, urn. Mt. Washington Glass Co. Circa 1888. Ref: H-1000 #49.

30. FROSTED CRANBERRY, bulb base, pulled flat fingers. Mt. Washington Glass Co. Circa 1890. Ref: H-R/U #1052.

31. HAT, ribbed, lustreless white. Mt. Washington Glass Co. Circa 1890.

32. FINE RIB, ball base, blue dot beads on top. Mt. Washington Glass Co. Circa 1890. Ref: H-R/U #1022 and #1052.

33. FINE RIB, tri-corner. Mt. Washington Glass Co. Milk with simulated Burmese finish inside.

34. HAT, lustreless white. Mt. Washington Glass Co. Circa 1890.

35. FIG MOLD, unfired Burmese, satin finish. Mt. Washington Glass Co. Circa 1880's. Ref: H-1000 #2.

36. SWIRLED TINY FINGERS, lustreless white. Mt. Washington Glass Co. Circa 1890. An almost identical unfired Burmese holder was not photographed. Ref: H-1000 #22 for shape.

37. FIG MOLD, Royal Flemish, pulled tiny fingers, vaseline satin with top and flower decoration. Mt. Washington Glass Co. Circa 1888.

38. SIMPLE SCROLL, pulled tiny fingers. Mt. Washington Glass Co. Circa 1888. Ref: H-1000 #59 and #91.

39. FIG MOLD, Royal Flemish. Mt. Washington Glass Co. Circa 1888. Ref: H-1000 #88.

40. SIMPLE SCROLL. Mt. Washington Glass Co. Circa 1888. Ref: H-1000 #59 and #91.

41. SIMPLE SCROLL, decorated milk glass, marked. Mt. Washington Glass Co. Circa 1888. Ref: H-1000 #55 and #59.

42. SWIRL MOLD, flared top. Mt. Washington Glass Co. Circa 1890. Ref: H-1000 #24.

43. SPIDER WEB, flared top, lustreless white (some have color stain on rim). Mt. Washington Glass Co. Circa 1890-1895. Ref: H-1000 #30 and #40; HR/U #1055.

44. SWIRL MOLD, round top. Mt. Washington Glass Co. Circa 1890. Ref: H-1000 #41 and #42.

45. URN. Simulated (painted) Burmese. Mt. Washington Glass Co.

46. SPIDER WEB, lustreless white, blue dot beads on top. Mt. Washington Glass Co. Circa 1890. Ref: H-1000 #30 and #40; H-R/U #1055.

47. ART GLASS, square shape, candy ribbon top holder in silverplate frame. Possibly English.

48. ART GLASS, pink cased holder mounted on silverplate pedestal. Probably European.

49. ART GLASS, Mother of Pearl, Diamond Quilt, bulbous base, crimp top holder in silverplate frame. Probably Thomas Webb & Sons.

50. ART GLASS, satin finish with hand decorated flowers similar to Coralene. Probably English.

51. ART GLASS, vaseline opalescent. Identified by Wm. Heacock as English. Typical English color and shape.

52. ART GLASS, Mother of Pearl, Diamond Quilt. Possibly Thomas Webb & Sons or Mt. Washington. This type of glass has been massively reproduced. The cased lining of the early pieces tends to be a thin, opaque white, while the newer items have a heavy, thick lining.

53. QUEEN MARY, Mother of Pearl, Diamond Quilt. Possibly Thomas Webb & Sons or Mt. Washington, circa 1890's. See information on #52 above. Ref: H-R/U #1075.

54. UPRIGHT FLOWER FORM holder in metal frame. Typical of English work. Circa 1890. Ref: H-1000 #528.

55. ART GLASS, amber lower half with ruby ruffled top half. Etched Bohemian type design.

56. ART GLASS, yellow and brown Art Deco style, maker unknown. Brass feet and rim. Possibly match or cigarette holder.

57. FRACTURED FOIL (NBW) At least three patents were issued to 19th century English and French glassmakers to stretch foil encased between two layers of glass. In France, Chine Metallique was made by Monot and Stumpf. In England, Silveria was developed by John Northwood for Stevens and Williams. Rigaree, as shown here, was typically English.

58. ART GLASS, blue enameled holder in silverplate frame. Maker unknown.

59. ART GLASS, cranberry holder in brass frame on marble base.

60. ART GLASS, cased, stretched Millefiori-type. Thorny crystal legs. Probably English, late 19th or early 20th century.

61. DAISY AND BUTTON BOAT, silverplate frame. A similar holder is shown in Ref: H-R/U page 94. Boat without the frame is shown in Ref: H/J-Salts.

62. ART GLASS, Fireglow in brass holder. Fireglow is brownish translucent glass that is firey when held to a light. Also known in blue, undecorated. Probably circa 1890's and European.

63. PANSY. Consolidated Lamp & Glass Co., Fostoria, Ohio, circa 1895. Made in opaque colors of white, green turquoise blue, light pink, dark pink and mixed pink to white. Items are sometimes frosted and/or cased. Cut off salt shakers and miniature lamps are nearly identical to the toothpick holders.

64. QUILT (OMN) aka FLORETTE (Wm. Heacock) aka BULGING PETALS (A. Peterson). Consolidated Lamp &

Glass Co. Fostoria, Ohio, circa 1885. Known in pink, mauve, bright green, three shades of blue, yellow, white, red satin, pigeon blood, apricot stain and clear. Colors may mix with white and the finish may be frosted or shiny. Items may or may not be cased. FLORETTE (see 978) is a very similar but different pattern, known only in salt shakers. It looks flatter and the flowers are more squarish. (Ref: *Pioneer*, newsletter of the Antique and Art Glass Salt Shaker Collectors Assn.) Beware of ground down shakers. Ref: H-1 #'s 112-115.

65. ART GLASS. Pink and white spatter satin glass with flower and leaf design. Decoration over spatter is unusual.

66. NORTHWOOD'S AURORA (OMN) aka BULBOUS RING NECK, RING NECK OPTIC, HOBB'S OPTIC and PRIMA DONNA. Northwood Glass Co., Martins Ferry, Ohio, circa 1890. Color is a vasa murrhina or cranberry spatter with mica flakes, called Royal Silver by Northwood. Also made in other Northwood colors. Ref: HMW-NOR; H-1 #37.

67. LEAF UMBRELLA. Northwood. Yellow, satin finished, cased. Made in other Northwood colors. Ref: H-l #'s 176-179 and HMW-NOR.

68. QUILTED PHLOX. Northwood, circa 1896. An unusual pinkish-mauve. Made in other Northwood colors. Ref: H-1 #'s 246 and 247 and HMW-NOR.

69. RIBBED OPAL LATTICE. Probably Northwood at Martin's Ferry, Ohio, circa early 1890's. Cranberry with satin finish. Made in other Northwood colors. Ref: H-1 #'s 198-200; H-9 page 57 and HMW-NOR.

70. SWIRL & LEAF. Northwood. Cased glass. White inner lining, pink and clear over that. Circa 1895-1900. Ref: HMW-NOR.

71, 72, 73. CROCODILE TEARS. Northwood/National/Dugan, circa 1900. Shown in blue, mauve and turquoise. Also made in other Northwood colors. Ref: H-1000 #131; H-1, p. 50; and HMW-NOR.

74. LEAF UMBRELLA. Northwood, circa 1889. Cranberry/white spatter with satin finish. Made in other Northwood colors. Ref: H-1 #'s 176-179 and HMW-NOR.

75. GUTTATE. Consolidated Lamp & Glass Co., circa 1885. Cased pink, satin finish. See #64 above (QUILT) for color information. Ref: H-1 #'s 135-137.

76, 77. LEAF MOLD. Northwood, circa 1891. Yellow-green satin and tortoise shell spatter (cranberry, white, vaseline, and dark burgundy). Ref: H-1 #'s 169-175 and HMW-NOR.

78. PARIAN SWIRL. Northwood, circa 1895. Cranberry satin with floral decoration. Made in other Northwood colors. Ref: H-1 #'s 228 and 229 and HMW-NOR.

79. AMBERINA. Bulge base, square top, Diamond Quilt. Probably Mt. Washington. 3" high.

80. AMBERINA URN. Venetian Diamond holder in James W. Tufts frame #3084, circa 1886. Ref: H-1 #314.

81. AMBERINA. Square top, straight sides, Venetian Diamond holder. New England Glass Works of W.L. Libbey & Sons, circa 1886. Silverplate frame by Wm. Rogers Mfg. of Hartford, Conn. Ref: H-1000 #555.

82. REVERSE AMBERINA. Pedestalled, Diamond Quilt. Similar to H-1000 #15, which is Inverted Thumbprint. Possibly Hobbs or Mt. Washington/Pairpoint, circa 1890.

83. ALEXANDRITE HAT. Webb, circa 1890's.

84. AMBERINA. Tri-cornered, Venetian Diamond. Probably Mt. Washington, circa 1885.

85. AMBERINA HAT. Probably Mt. Washington or New England Glass Co., circa 1885-1890.

86. AMBERINA. Pie crust rim, Diamond Quilted inside with vertical rib outside. Probably Mt. Washington. Similar to Ref: H-R/U #1098.

87. CRANBERRY FLASHED. Decorated, typical of Moser, late 19th century.

88. AMBERINA. Inverted Thumbprint, bulge base. Possibly English. Reproductions reportedly being imported. Ref: H-1000 #'s 124, 148 and 290 and notes in Ref: H-R/U page 5.

89. CRANBERRY TO CLEAR. Striped, inside ribbed. Maker unknown.

90. FROSTED RUBINA. Flower decoration. Possibly Mt. Washington of the 1880 period.

91. DAISY & BUTTON BOAT. Amberina. Probably Hobbs, Brockunier & Co., circa 1890. Holder is Tufts No.2600. Known in apple green. Probably available in the usual blue, amber and crystal colors. Ref: H-R/U page 96.

92. CRANBERRY FLASHED CRYSTAL. Base and lower portions ground and polished. Scene painted in black on flat gold. Probably Moser, 1945-1950.

93. ZIPPERED CORNER. Possibly Northwood. Ref: H-GC 6.

94. INVERTED THUMBPRINT. Cranberry, in silverplate frame by Aurora Silverplate Co.

95. OPTIC TUBE (NBW). Cranberry flashed. Silverplate frame with foreign markings.

96. THORNY TREE TRUNK. Freeform cranberry opalescent. Probably Stevens and Williams, circa 1890. Ref: H-1000 #861 is similar.

97. INVERTED THUMBPRINT. Bulge base, cranberry, possibly English (shape reproduced; see #88).

98. MARY GREGORY TYPE. Bulbous body. Date uncertain. Reportedly appeared in a retail catalog, Jenning's Red Barn, in 1979.

99. INVERTED THUMBPRINT. Cranberry cased over amber glass. Ref: H-R/U #1014.

100. INVERTED THUMBPRINT. Bulge base variant, cranberry cased over vaseline. Age uncertain.

101. ART GLASS. Blown cranberry with silver overlay. Probably European. Age uncertain.

102. CRISS-CROSS. Consolidated Lamp & Glass Co., Fostoria, Ohio, circa 1894. Ref: H-1 #191-193.

103. SKIRTED OPTIC. Probably Mt. Washington Glass Co., circa 1885-1890. See Ref: H-R/U #'s 1088, 1097, and 1113; and H-1000 #42 for shape.

104. WIDE SWIRL (NBW). Bulge base, cranberry opalescent. Also known in blue opalescent. See #249.

105. NORTHWOOD'S AURORA (OMN) aka RING NECK OPTIC, BULBOUS RING NECK, HOBBS OPTIC and PRIMA DONNA. Etched rubina. Ref: HMW-NOR and H-1 #37 and #214.

106. SHRINER'S SOUVENIR 1907. Embossed with Pittsburgh, Syria Temple, four names and Los Angeles, 1907. Originally produced as a bar glass.

107. INVERTED THUMBPRINT. Square top, straight sides, rubina. Probably New England Glass Co., circa 1890. Ref: H-R/U page 5.

108. RING BASE MOLD. Cranberry, opalescent diamonds. Heacock called this pattern Opalescent Diamonds (H-9 page 53) and, in his text on geometric patterns, states this was probably made by Phoenix Glass Co., circa 1884-1885. In H-R/U, page 5, the update on the Ring Base mold says that this shape is "probably Mt. Washington." Research continues.

109. BURMESE. Pink lining is color stained. Probably Webb, circa 1888. Ref: H-1000 #80.

110. QUEEN MARY. Pink cased, satin finish. Probably Webb. Ref: H-R/U #1075 and H-1000 #60.

111. GLOSSY PEACHBLOW. Piecrust rim, pink to white cased glass. Age and maker uncertain.

112. MOTHER OF PEARL. Diamond Quilt, crystal rim. Probably Webb, circa 1895.

113-114. MOTHER OF PEARL. Moire' pattern, cased, frosted, with duck bill feet. Probably European. Age uncertain.

115. BULB BASE. Square top, cased, pink lining. Probably Webb.

116. MOTHER OF PEARL - RIBBON. Yellow, satin glass, unusual shape. Probably European. Believed to be of recent origin.

117. BURMESE. Bulb base, fluted rim, glossy finish. Marked "Queens Burmese Ware, Thos. Webb, Patented R 8016 T". Circa 1886.

118. RING BASE. Mother of Pearl Raindrop. Shape would indicate Mt. Washington, but there is some question about age. Research on this shape and this type of glass continues. Ref: H-R/U #1009.

119. MOTHER OF PEARL. Diamond Quilt. Maker unknown. Top may have been ground down. Age uncertain.

120. CURTAIN TOP OVERLAY. Bristol glass, blue. Circa 1895. Ref: H-1000 #119.

121. SQUATTY BULB VARIANT (NBW). Known in green, dark ruby, clear and possibly other color stains with silver overlays. Probably European.

122. CUT GLASS. Marked "Hawkes". Similar to H-R/U #1019 and #1020.

123. RUFFLED TOP. Bristol-type blue glass. Probably European, circa 1920's.

124. AMERICAN BEAUTY ROSE (NBH). Ribbon, Mother of Pearl, satin glass. Probably European, believed to be of recent origin.

125. ART GLASS. Orange satin with poppy decoration. Probably foreign, likely to be Czech.

126. HAT. Diamond Quilt, glossy custard color. Very similar to Mt. Washington in appearance, but believed to be a recent Pairpoint/Bryden issue.

127. HAT. Marked "VASART", by Strathern Glass Co., Crieff, Scotland. Rose colored base shades to blue rim, with gold mica flecks. Ref: BOUL-TP plate 268.

128. HAT. Cased glass. Probably English circa 1890. Ref: L-VG plate 143 and H-1000 #118.

129. HAT. Peachblow, optic ribs. New England Glass Co., circa 1893. Ref: H-R/U #1064.

130. POMONA. Tri-corner, small, first grind, amber stain. New England Glass Co., circa 1885.

131. POMONA. Tri-corner, Midwestern, small with unusual lavender lustre top. Circa 1890.

132. POMONA. Tri-corner, first grind, larger than 131, with amber stain. New England Glass Co., circa 1885.

133. WEBB-TYPE PEACHBLOW. Ball base, satin finish. Authorities could not agree on attribution or age.

134. BULB BASE. Square top. The shape and color suggest Thomas Webb & Sons as the maker. Circa 1890's. Ref: H-R/U pages 5 & 6.

135. CORALENE. Tri-corner. Decorated with tiny glass beads. Age and maker uncertain.

136. THREADED DIAMOND QUILT. Rubina Verde. Widely produced in the U.S. and Europe. Part of liqueur set. Age uncertain.

137. BULBOUS. Cranberry, blown with enamel decoration. The decor is of the lacy enamel type attributed as being French, circa 1905-1910. Ref: H/J-Salts.

138. ALEXANDRITE. Thomas Webb & Sons, circa 1900. Beware of reproductions. Ref: R-19CG.

139. ART GLASS. Satin finished, gold decorated. Maker unknown.

140. POMONA. Crimp neck, piecrust rim. New England Glass Co., circa 1887. Ref: H-1000 #52.

141. ART GLASS. Rosaline and alabaster. Unsigned. Origin, age and intended purpose uncertain.

142. ART GLASS. Pedestalled, cased, ruffled top. Typical of Webb's glass, but origin and age uncertain.

143. ART GLASS. Ruffled top with floral decoration. Typical of Webb glass, but origin and age uncertain.

144. TAPERED BULGE (NBW). Painted opal glass, Cabin in Snow. Three possibilities: (1) Made by Mt. Washington Glass Co., then painted by Smith Bros. decorating firm, circa 1888-1892. Ref: LCH-SAL1. (2) Made at Sandwich. Mary Gregory gave a similarly decorated item to her aunt in 1883. Ref: B/K-GIS. (3) Made at Sandwich. Decorated by Smith at Sandwich.

145. PAINTED MILK. Brown and yellow daisy. Possibly made at Sandwich, decorated by Smith.

146. GLOSSY AGATA (worn). Base glass is Peachblow. New England Glass Co., circa 1880's. The white line at the top is in the glass. Same shape as Ref: H-1000 #102 and H-R/U #1061.

147. GLOSSY AGATA. Square top, straight side. New England Glass Co., circa 1888. Ref: H-1000 #50.

148. DECORATED MILK GLASS. Ref: H-1000 #872, but this one looks shorter.

149. HAT. Milk glass, Mt. Washington, circa 1885-1890. Ref: H-1000 #62.

150. HAT. Milk glass, decorated. Mt. Washington Glass Co., circa 1885. Ref: H-1000 #62.

151. NAKARA. Match holder. Signed CFM Co. (C.F. Monroe). Circa 1890's. Ref: C-CFM page 126.

152. NAKARA. Match holder. C.F. Monroe, circa 1890's. Ref: C-CFM.

153, 154, 155. DECORATED BARREL aka EGG. Boston & Sandwich Glass Co., circa 1885. Attribution based on decorations. #153, the Autumn Leaves decor, has stems twisted together as did fragments dug at the factory site. Colors and themes are typical of Sandwich. Ref: H-R/U #'s 1358-1360 and H-1000 #378.

156. URN. Jade green, Steuben, marked No.2648. Circa 1916. Ref: S-AAG.

157. DAUM NANCY. Marked. Winter scene of church on one side, windmill on the other. 2" tall, 3 1/2" wide with handles.

158. CAMEO GLASS. Signed DeVez. St.Hilaire, Touzier, de Varreaux & Co., Pantin, France, circa 1900. Ref: R-19CG.

159. ART GLASS. Monet & Stumpf. Unmarked.

160. MILLEFIORE PAPERWEIGHT BASE, LUTZ-TYPE TOP. St. Louis, France. A similar item, identified as a pen holder is shown in *Collector's Paperweights* by Selman; however, this item is believed to be more recent Murano glass.

161. CAMEO GLASS. Signed Galle'. French, c. 1900.

162. DAUM NANCY. Marked. Amber frosted with gold leaves and enamelled flowers. Generally considered to be a shot glass, but actively sought by toothpick holder collectors. Ref: H-R/U #1105 and H-1000 #36.

163. GALLE'. Signed. 2" tall, 1 1/2" across top.

164. DAUM NANCY. Marked. Traditional toothpick holder shape with two handles.

165. THREE HANDLES. Unusual green to blue shading with orange enamel decoration and applied reeded handles. Probably European.

166. DAUM NANCY. Marked. Probably a small tumbler, but sought as a toothpick holder due to the beauty of the glass and decoration.

167. GALLE'. Marked. Cranberry overlay, cut to clear. Appears to be cameo.

168. DAUM NANCY. Marked. Possibly part of decanter set, proudly included in toothpick holder collection.

169. DAUM NANCY. Marked. Decor is brushed with gold.

170. GALLE'. Marked. Cameo glass.

171. DAUM NANCY. Unsigned, but typical shape and decoration for Daum Nancy.

172. ENGRAVED. Embossed ST. LOUIS on bottom. "Hotel Meurice" souvenir. Cut to clear. Possibly Crista Nories du Val St. Lambert. Ref: H-R/U #1020.

173. ART GLASS. Iridescent, amethyst, chased in spider web fashion. Attributed to Palme-Koenig.

174. ART GLASS. Blue Aurene. Steuben. Marked "Aurene" and "No. 1641".

175. ART GLASS. Tiffany Favrille. Consists of two pieces; 3 1/4" saucer and 2 3/8" high holder.

176. DOUBLE GOURD. Blue Aurene. Steuben. Marked "Aurene". Ref: BOUL-TP.

177. ART GLASS. Tiffany type. Good iridescence. Number on bottom, "0486-g" (or j).

178. ART GLASS. Urn shape, Steuben. Blue Aurene. Marked "Aurene No. 2648".

179. ART GLASS. Ruffled top. Blue Aurene. Steuben. Marked "Aurene No. 2640". Ref: H-R/U #1006; BOUL-TP plate 10.

180. ART GLASS. Dimpled. Signed "Quezal 7313". One side is double dimpled.

181. ART GLASS. Dimpled. Damascene decorated. Signed "Quezal". Ref: G-AGN.

182. ART GLASS. Optic panels. Tiffany. Marked "No. 698 LCT". Amber base glass with blue iridescence. Eight inner ribs.

183. ART GLASS. Optic panels, swirl shape. Tiffany. Signed "LCT W 1470". Purple highlights on rim.

184. ART GLASS. Quezal-type.

185. ART GLASS. Tiffany. Circa 1895. Signed "LCT, D2619". Ref: K-LCT and K-TAG.

186. ART GLASS. Tri-cornered. Pinch top. Signed "Quezal".

187. ART GLASS. Cone shape. Paperweight base. Tiffany. Marked "LCT Favrille #1301". Ref: BOUL-TP.

188. ART GLASS. Puffy base. Ruffled top. Resembles the Monot-Stumpf French art glass of the late 19th century. Ref: H/J - SALTS.

189. CONTEMPORARY ART GLASS. Signed "Terry Crider 1984." Jack-in-the-Pulpit style.

190. CONTEMPORARY ART GLASS. Signed "Terry Crider 1985." Jack-in-the-Pulpit style.

191. CONTEMPORARY ART GLASS. Signed "Terry Crider 1987." Jack-in-the-Pulpit style.

192. CONTEMPORARY ART GLASS. Signed "Terry Crider 1984." Jack-in-the-Pulpit style.

193. CONTEMPORARY ART GLASS. Signed "Terry Crider 1984."

194. CONTEMPORARY ART GLASS. Signed "Dominic Labino."

195. CONTEMPORARY ART GLASS. Lotton Art Glass. Mandarin Red color. Probably miniature vase.

196. CONTEMPORARY ART GLASS. Signed "Terry Crider 1977."

197. CONTEMPORARY ART GLASS. Signed "Terry Crider 1982."

198. CONTEMPORARY ART GLASS. Signed "Terry Crider 1981."

199. CONTEMPORARY ART GLASS. James Lundberg, California.

200. CONTEMPORARY ART GLASS. Lotton Art Glass. Gold Lustre color.

201. CONTEMPORARY ART GLASS. Signed "Terry Crider 1983."

202. CONTEMPORARY ART GLASS. Signed "Terry Crider 1985."

203. CONTEMPORARY ART GLASS. Signed "Terry Crider 1984."

204. CONTEMPORARY ART GLASS. Signed "Terry Crider 1984."

205. BLUE OPAQUE. New England Glass Co., circa 1886. Has ribbed optic effect. Color very rare. Ref: H-R/U #1053.

206. GREEN OPAQUE. New England Glass Co., circa 1886. Ref: H-R/U #1053.

207. GLOSSY BURMESE. Ruffled rim. Mt. Washington Glass Co., circa 1888. Ref: H-1000 #3 for shape.

208. FIG MOLD. Glossy Burmese. Mt. Washington Glass Co., circa 1888. Ref: H-1000 #2.

209. HAT. Milk Glass. Probably English. Hand painted, Delft design. Circa 1890's.

210. GLOSSY BURMESE. Wide mouth, Diamond Quilt. Mt. Washington Glass Co., circa 1888. May have been made for other than toothpicks.

211. PARALLEL GREEK KEY. Unfired Burmese. Mt. Washington Glass Co., circa 1888. Ref: H-1000 #33.

212. GLOSSY BURMESE. Diamond Quilt, straight sides. Mt. Washington Glass Co., circa 1888.

213. CONTEMPORARY ART GLASS. Threaded decoration. Iridized. Signed "Terry Crider, 1977, NTHCS."

214. CONTEMPORARY ART GLASS. Lotton Art Glass, circa 1980's. "Pulled feather" or "pin hook" design.

215. CONTEMPORARY ART GLASS. "King Tut", Lotton Art Glass. Signed "John Lotton, 1991". "Pulled feather" or "pin hook" design.

216. CONTEMPORARY ART GLASS. Lotton Art Glass. Threaded decoration. Circa 1990.

217. CONTEMPORARY ART GLASS. Cameo glass marked "Kelsey/Pilgrim". Pilgrim Glass Co., circa 1991.

218. CONTEMPORARY ART GLASS. "Leafy", cameo glass, signed "John Lotton." Lotton Art Glass Co., circa 1991.

219. CONTEMPORARY ART GLASS. Cameo glass, marked "Kelsey/Pilgrim". Pilgrim Glass Co., circa 1991.

220. CONTEMPORARY ART GLASS. Cameo glass, marked "Kelsey/Pilgrim". Sailboat design on reverse. Pilgrim Glass Co., circa 1990.

221. INVERTED THUMBPRINT. Enamel decorations. Gold rim and base. Probably foreign. Also see No. 310.

222. THREE HANDLED. Clear, eight panels, gold trimmed. Enamel decoration. Probably European. See No. 327.

223. MARY GREGORY TYPE. Made in Europe and U.S. since 1880's. Probably European. Possibly more recent.

224. ZIPPER SLASH. Enamel decoration. George Duncan & Sons, circa 1891. Ref: H-1 #'s 335 and 336; H-1000 #'s 226 and 233.

225. CO-OP'S ROYAL. Cooperative Flint Glass Co., circa 1894 to 1915. Probably early 1900's with this treatment.

226. ZIPPER SLASH. See No. 224 above.

227. MOSER. Applied glass beads. Fern pattern.

228. CLOISONNE-LIKE. Blown, inlaid Cloisonne type flowers in light green base glass. Layer of clear glass covering. European.

229. PLIQUE-A-JOUR. Process involves translucent enamel without a backing, framed within metal work. Metal in this case is gold. European.

230. INVERTED THUMBPRINT. Cranberry flashed (note the clear layer of glass visible at the base). Probably English, circa 1900. Ref: H-R/U #1013.

231. ART GLASS. Amber with a hunting scene decal. Maker and date unknown.

232. INVERTED THUMBPRINT. Ring base mold. Deep cobalt blue. Possibly Mt. Washington Glass Co., but questions continue to arise regarding this shape. Research continues. Ref: H-R/U page 5.

233. CLOISONNE. Tumbler shape. Probably Chinese.

234. CLOISONNE. 1 1/2" across top, 2" high. Probably Chinese.

235. METAL. Probably brass, with enamel design. Probably Chinese.

236. METAL. Silver with enamel decoration. Possibly an American attempt at the art of Cloisonne, or could be Chinese. 2 1/8" high.

237. TOKYO. Jefferson No.212. Jefferson Glass Co. of Steubenville, Ohio. Plain and opalescent colors of crystal, blue, vaseline, and a more bluish green. May be decorated with gold. Ref: H-1 # 309 and 310.

238. LATE WESTMORELAND aka WESTMORELAND, NEW WESTMORELAND. Westmoreland Glass Co., circa 1898. Made in clear, teal blue and emerald green, sometimes with gold decoration. Ref: H-R/U #1177.

239. COLONIAL STAIRSTEPS. Speculative attribution to Northwood Glass Co., circa 1906. Found in light blue, clear and a very light aqua, sometimes with opalescence. Ref: H-2 #576. See also 973.

240. IDYLL. Jefferson Glass Co. #251, circa 1907. Made in electric blue, light blue, apple green, clear, and canary (vaseline). May be plain or opalescent. Sometimes gold trimmed. Ref: H-1 #149-150.

241. RING BASE. Spatter glass with overshot. Research on this shape continues. Ref: H-R/U page 5 and examples in H-R/U and H-1000.

242. FLORIDA aka SUNKEN PRIMROSE. Greensburg Glass Co., circa 1893. Colors include emerald green, a light canary opalescent, at least two ruby stain variations, clear and clear with frosted flowers. Ref: H-1 #116.

243. LOCKET ON CHAIN. A.H. Heisey Co. #160, circa 1900-1902. Emerald green with gold. Also found in crystal, canary and an all-over ruby stain with gold trim. Ref: H-1000 #228.

244. RING BASE. Spatter glass. Research on this shape continues. Ref: H-R/U page 5 and examples in H-R/U and H-1000.

245. SCROLL WITH ACANTHUS. H. Northwood and Co. at Wheeling, W.Va., circa 1903. Colors known include this blue, clear, very light apple green, and varying shades of purple slag. The transparent ones may be decorated with gold, enamel dots, or cranberry stain. Ref: H-1 #277-279.

246. COLUMNED THUMBPRINTS. Westmoreland Glass Co., circa 1902-1905. Found only in clear, sometimes with dots of magenta, blue, green or yellow. Ref: H-R/U #1180.

247. NATIONAL (OMN) aka S-REPEAT. National Glass Co., Northwood Works, when run by Dugan. Circa 1903. Made in clear, apple green, blue, green and amethyst with very limited production in opalescent colors. Many reproductions, some of which are difficult to detect. Ref: H-1 #290 and #291.

248. NESTOR. National Glass Co., Northwood Works, run by Dugan, circa 1903. Design of tiny leaves, flowers and vines accompanies the enamel scroll. Colors include blue, apple green, crystal and amethyst. Ref: H-1 #'s 185 and 353.

249. WIDE SWIRL (NBW). Bulge Base. Could be European or American. Also see No. 104.

250. IRIS WITH MEANDER aka IRIS. Jefferson Glass Co., circa 1904. Known in crystal, blue, green, amethyst, and opalescent colors of white, blue, green, canary and this dark aqua. Ref: H-1 #154-158.

251. SEAWEED. Opalescent. Originally Heacock reported production by Hobbs, Northwood and Beaumont. The Northwood book covering the 1890's period did not include it. Known colors are cranberry, blue and white opalescent. Ref: H-1 #202, text in H-9 and text in HMW-NOR.

252. CUT BLOCK. A.H. Heisey Co., circa 1896. Clear, ruby stain and amber stain. Ref: Ref: H-1 #71.

253. RABBIT MATCH. U.S. Glass Co., circa 1893. Clear and clear with ruby stain. Reproduced in many colors with scalloped top on basket. Ref: H-1000 #751 and page 103.

254. U.S.A. U.S. Glass Co., circa 1901. Clear, clear with ruby stain, and pale marigold lustre finish; often found with advertising on base. Ref: H-1000 #669.

255. BRILLIANT aka RIVERSIDE #436 and PETALLED MEDALLION. Riverside Glass Works, Wellsburg, West Virginia, circa 1895. Clear, ruby stain, and amber stain. Ref: H-1 #35.

256. PEEK-A-BOO. McKee Glass Co. after 1900. Made over the years with several variations on the top and base. The old one has a hole in the bottom that goes up into the stem. Those made in the 1940's and later are cupped on the bottom. Ref: H-1000 #735.

257. DIAMOND WAFFLE aka U.S. DIAMOND BLOCK. U.S. Glass Co., #15025, circa 1891. Clear, ruby stain, and rare in emerald green. Ref: H-R/U #1233.

258. KENTUCKY. U.S. Glass Co. #15051, circa 1890. Known in clear, emerald green, cobalt blue and clear with ruby stain. Ref: H-1 #161.

259. SWINGER aka MADOLIN and MADOLINE (OMN). Originally made by Cooperative Flint Glass Co., circa 1893. In the 1940's, 50's, 60's and maybe even later, Ralston Westlake of Columbus, Ohio applied ruby stain to items made by Fenton Glass Co. He sometimes cut designs, such as the one pictured here, into the glass. This design is frequently seen on the BUTTON ARCHES pattern. SWINGER is usually decorated with enamel flowers, a decal transfer, ruby stain and/or gold. Ref: H-1000 #302 is probably old. H-1000 #251 shape is dated 1922 and is known dated 1939. H-1000 #303 is probably a later example.

260. MILLARD. U.S. Glass Co. #15016, circa 1893-1895. Also found in clear and amber stain. Sometimes etched. Ref: H-1 pages 50 and 52; H-1000 #231; and H-7 #43.

261. JUNO aka STAR WHORL and DOUBLE PINWHEEL. Indiana Glass Co. at Dunkirk, Indiana, circa 1908. Clear and clear with ruby stain. Ref: H-R/U #1306.

262. THUMBNAIL aka FLAT TO ROUND PANEL. Duncan & Miller Glass Co. #73, circa 1909-1913. Clear, clear with gold, ruby stain, and clear with silver overlay. Ref: H-1000 #672.

263. PRISCILLA or Dalzell's Alexis (OMN). Dalzell, Gilmore & Leighton Co., circa 1892. Clear and ruby stain. Ref: H-1000 #603.

264. INDIANA'S COLONIAL. Indiana Glass Co. of Dunkirk, Indiana. Widely reissued in the 1970's or early 1980's in clear and in amber by Tiara Exclusives. All amber is considered reissue. Ref: H-R/U #1254.

265. ZIPPER EDGE PANELS. Duncan & Miller Glass Co. #46, circa 1905. Clear and ruby stain only. Ref: H-R/U #1242.

266. DANDELION. Fostoria Glass Co. #1819, circa 1911. Clear and rare in ruby stain. Ref: H-1000 #635.

267. ALEXANDER (NBW). This souvenir says "Mr. Alexander Supt. Priveledges, West Alexander Fair, 1905." The town of West Alexander is on the Ohio-Pennsylvania line just north of I-70. Ref: M-TP Plate XXVI, row 4, #1 shows a similar holder.

268. BUCKINGHAM. U.S. Glass Co. #15106, circa 1907. Clear and clear with rose and green stain. Ref: H-1000 #737.

269. TEPEE aka DUNCAN #28, ARIZONA and NEMESIS. George A. Duncan & Sons at Washington, Pa., circa 1896. Clear and with ruby or amber stain. Ref: H-1 page 50 and 52.

270. RIVERSIDE aka THE DERBY. Riverside Glass Co., circa 1897. Clear and rare in vaseline. Another version is flared out and the lower part is more square in shape. Ref: H-1000 #634.

271. BEADED GRAPE aka CALIFORNIA. U.S. Glass Co. #15059, circa 1895. Made in clear and emerald green. This one is decorated with purple, green and yellow stain. Ref: H-1 #20.

272. WINGED SCROLL. A.H. Heisey Co., circa 1901. Produced in Ivorina Verde (a light custard), clear, emerald green, ivory, opal and vaseline (canary). Similar item with straight sides is a match holder. Ref: H-1 #325; and J-HTP page 55.

273. GENEVA. Probably by Northwood, circa 1900, and later by McKee Glass Co. Made in pale custard, emerald green, clear and chocolate. Decorated with brown stain or green stain (fired on) with gold trim (by Northwood) and sometimes green and red stain (by McKee). Ref: H-1 #126-128; and HMW-NOR page 126 and 141.

274. SUNSET. Dithridge & Co. #50, circa 1894. Opaque colors of white, pink, custard yellow, blue and green, sometimes decorated with gold or with a satin finish. Ref: H-1 #295.

275. SHELL & SEAWEED. Consolidated Lamp & Glass Co., circa 1894. Known in white milk, cased blue, cased pink, cased yellow, decorated milk, and opaque colors of pink, blue and green. Ref: H-R/U #1161 and H-1 #358.

276. TOKYO. Jefferson Glass Co. #212, circa 1904. Plain and opalescent colors of clear, blue and green, sometimes decorated with gold. Ref: H-1 #309-310.

277. DIAMOND SPEARHEAD. National Glass Company, Northwood Works at Indiana, Pa., circa 1900. Made in clear and opalescent colors of clear, vaseline, green and two shades of blue. Opalescent colors are more readily available than clear. Ref: H-1 #74-77.

278. PORTLAND. U.S. Glass Co. #15121, circa 1900-1910. Made in clear, color stained, and apple green. Ref: H-1000 #674.

279. BEADED PANEL & SUNBURST. A.H. Heisey Co. #1235, circa 1897-1908. Made only in crystal with decoration added later. This lustre finish is pale marigold and is not fired. Other decorations are ruby stain, green, gold, bronze and various combinations of the above. Ref: H-1 #22; H-R/U page 69 and J-HTP page 25.

280. IDYLL. Jefferson Glass Co. #251, circa 1907. Made in electric blue, light blue, apple green, clear, and canary (vaseline). May be plain or opalescent. Sometimes gold trimmed. Ref: H-1 #149-150.

281. SWAG WITH BRACKETS. Jefferson Glass Co., circa 1903. Colors include deep blue, amethyst, green, an odd yellow-green, and opalescent colors of white, blue, green, and canary (vaseline). Massively reproduced by Degenhart in many colors. Old ones have smooth, rounded points on the top and a square shaped bracket. Newer ones usually have sharp points on the top and a sort of T-shaped bracket. Ref: H-1 #297-300.

282. RIBBED THUMBPRINT. Jefferson Glass Co. #221, circa 1907. Made in clear, ruby stained for souvenir ware, custard and electric blue. Ref: H-1 #254 and 356.

283. SULTAN (OMN) aka WILD ROSE WITH SCROLLING. A toy spoon holder by McKee Glass Co., circa 1910-1920. Colors of clear, frosted clear, green, chocolate and blue. Ref: H-1 #323-324; H-1000 #105 and 284; and W-PGAM.

284. FRAMED LOOP (Name by Arnison). European. 3" high, recess is 2 1/4" deep.

285. OPALINE. Marked "Baccarat." Late 19th or early 20th century.

286. FOOTED DEVIL (NBW). Marked "SV". Three sheaves of wheat and 3 devil faces with donkey ears, horns and beards. Possibly a characterization of Mephistopheles. Probably European.

287. FRENCH PANELS (NBW). Clambroth. Probably Baccarat. Also known in blue and with other decorations.

288. OPALINE. Possibly St. Louis, France.

289. SHELL & SCALE. Shown in NTHCS *Toothpick Bulletin*, June 1985. Known only in light yellow custard. Ref: P-GSS

290. MICHIGAN. U.S. Glass Co., circa 1900-1910. Shown here with blue stain and enamel decor. Ref: H-1000 #'s 237, 259, and 260.

291. ART GLASS. Mold blown glass, applied ribbon of blue glass. Studio artist type item. Possibly English. Maker and date unknown.

292. HEART. Dithridge & Co., circa 1894. Also made in opaque pink, white, yellow custard and pink/white. Ref: H-1 #246-247.

293. QUILTED PHLOX. Northwood/National/Dugan. Circa 1896-1903. Opaque colors of blue, white, pink, green and mauve and these are sometimes cased. Also produced in transparent emerald green, apple green, light blue and amethyst. Ref: H-1 #246-247; and HMW-NOR pages 95, 126-127.

294. HOOPED BARREL VARIANT (NBW). Maker and date unknown. Ref: Similar to H-1000 #94.

295. GRECIAN COLUMN. Circa 1890-1896. Known colors are milk, light blue opaque, pink opaque and cased mauve. Probably made at Fostoria, Ohio. Ref: H-R/U #1155.

296. 1903 SHRINER'S SOUVENIR N0.2 (NBW). Markings include "Syria, Pittsburgh, 1903", and "Los Angeles".

297. PALM LEAF. Consolidated Lamp & Glass Co., circa 1894. Made in this satin finish blue, shiny colors of blue, white, pink, white with pink highlights, and yellow. Ref: H-1 #223.

298. CUT GLASS. Light violet color.

299. HUB (Name by Boyd). Known in blue, yellow, amber and green, all lightened in intensity by being frosted. The colors suggest depression age. Called HUB because the design is similar to the center of a wagon wheel.

300. SWIRL & ROSETTE (NBW). Made by Sowerby. See H-R/U, p. 92.

301. UMBRELLA STAND (NBW). Maker and age unknown. Probably foreign. In the 1880's, Duncan made a similar Daisy & Button pattern with a handle, both with and without a stand.

302. MADAME BOVARY. French. Circa 1900. Ref: H-R/U #1011.

303. CROWNED FLOWERS (NBW). Believed to be English slag or marble glass, circa 1880's.

304. QUEEN VICTORIA. Webb Peachblow, circa 1890. Satin finish. Ref: H-R/U #1070.

305. ART GLASS. Moser type. Probably European.

306. FOOTED BALL (NBW). Webb, circa 1890. The referenced holder has a ruffled top. Ref: BOUL-TP, plate 41.

307. PANELLED TULIPS (NBW). Sowerby & Co. #1185, Ellison Glass Works, Gateshead on Tyne England. Circa 1881. Ref: H-R/U page 92.

308. BRISTOL TYPE. Quality glass with fine, highly detailed enamel design. Probably European. Ref: Toothpick Bulletin, May, 1987.

309. ART GLASS. Possibly French. Blue opaline, gold decoration.

310. BLOWN. Enamel decorations. The decor suggests a foreign maker, probably English.

311. BRISTOL. Cased pink. Glossy around center band, but frosted elsewhere. Enamel decoration. Probably English.

312. RAINBOW. Stevens & Williams, England. Blown glass. Part of a table set, circa 1890.

313. FLOWER DELIGHT (NBW). Cased rose, with white lining and outer layer of crystal rigaree. Probably English, circa 1890's.

314. HOBNAIL. Probably European. Blue-green with amethyst flashing sometimes called "blue amberina." Color combination leads some to believe it might be Webb.

315. ART GLASS. Blown. Hand painted flowers. European, circa 1915-1920.

316. CUT, ART DECO. Base is rectangular, top has six sides. Two plain panels, two etched with tree and bird, and two etched with seagulls. Probably Czech.

317. CUT, ART DECO. Oblong, eight panels, three each front and back. Each long side has a pyramid of circles. Probably European.

318. CUT, ART DECO. Made by Kolloman/Moser. Black enamel on clear. "Bronkit-Black Miello".

319. CUT, ART DECO. Ruby overlay, cut to clear. Probably European.

320. CUT, ART DECO. This appears to be polished surfaces. Probably 1920's. Maker unknown.

321. CUT, ART DECO. Amber cut to clear. Base marked "Sterling Silver" and "Germany".

322. ART DECO. Eight sided with silver deposit flower on four panels and silver on stepped sides.

323. CUT, ART DECO. Made by Kolloman/Moser. "Bronkit", Black Miello decoration. Probably small vase.

324. ART GLASS. Pink Opaline, heavy gold. Possibly French. Possibly Moser.

325. ART GLASS. Probably Moser. Highly decorated. Marked "2647". Ref: Decor similar to H-R/U #1084.

326. BULGE BASE. Bluina. Moser type decoration. Ref: BC-AG plate 84 for decoration. Shape and color are like H-1000 #148.

327. CLEAR. Enamel decoration. Good quality European glass. The inscribed number, "4603/228" is a Moser type code - four digit shape followed by three digit decor. Also see #222.

328. CRACKLE GLASS. Applied prunts. Glass characteristics suggest Blenko or Viking, perhaps of recent vintage. The painted decoration suggests 1950's or 1960's. European is another opinion.

329. ART GLASS. Iridized crystal. Loetz type, probably European.

330. ART GLASS. Probably Moser. See Plate 129 in *Ludwig Moser* by M.K. Charon for decoration.

331. ART GLASS. Amber holder decorated with gold and white enamel dots. Applied blue glass feet continue up sides to form handles. Possibly Moser. Ref: Similar to H-R/U #1084.

332. HAND VASE. Fenton No. 38, circa 1942-44. 3 5/8" high. Blue opalescent. Reissue mid-1980's doesn't flare as much, is lighter in color, and has a disc added to the base to make a stepped pedestal. Blue, clear and vaseline opalescent, and probably other Fenton colors. Ref: H-FEN2.

333. FROG TOOTHPICK (OMN). Shown in 1911 Cooperative Flint Glass Co. advertisement. See #335. Ref: H-R/U page 85.

334. CAT TOOTHPICK aka CAT ON A PILLOW. Daisy & Button. Amber, blue, vaseline and clear. Circa 1885-1905. Beware of reproductions. Ref: H-1 #88 and H-1000 page 103.

335. FROG TOOTHPICK (OMN). Shown in 1911 Cooperative Flint Glass Co. advertisement. See #333. Ref: H-R/U page 85.

336. DARWIN. Richards & Hartley, circa 1888-1895 with production continued by U.S. Glass Co. Clear, amber, blue and a light vaseline.

337. POINTED PANELS WITH OVALS (NBW). Possibly French or other European maker. Circa 1890's.

338. RIBBED DAISY BAND. Clear, blue and probably other colors. Ref: BOUL-TP plate 191.

339. STUMP (OMN) aka BIRD IN STUMP. McKee Glass Co., circa 1885. Also sold with lid as a mustard jar. Light blue, amber, vaseline and clear. Tip of beak is missing in photo. Ref: H-R/U page 91; H-1000 #756.

340. ALLIGATOR aka CROCODILE. Circa 1890. Light blue, amber, vaseline, milk and clear. Called candle holder and match safe in advertisement. Ref: H-1000 #324; H-R/U page 89.

341. HEXAGONAL INVERTED THUMBPRINT. Circa 1895. Blue, reverse amberina, amber and probably other colors. Ref: HR/U #1016.

342. FREE FORM THREE LOBE. Floral decoration.

343. BULGE BASE. Inverted Thumbprint. Research on this shape continues. Age and maker uncertain. Ref: H-1000 #'s 124, 148, and 290.

344. D & B BOTTOM (NBW). The Daisy & Button pattern appears in the bottom of this holder.

345. SIX PANEL FLARE (NBW). May be a shot glass.

346. RINGED SCOOP (NBW). Age and maker unknown.

347. FIVE CENT PAIL (NBW). Circa 1890. Described as "5 cent colored glass pail for matches or toothpicks" in a Butler Bros. advertisement. Ref: H-R/U page 89.

348. TOBOGGAN SHOE. Cane pattern. Probably Bryce Bros., circa 1880's. Clear, amber and blue novelty item. Crossed snowshoes on front are not visible here. Ref: Y-SG.

349. STARS AND BARS WITH LEAF. Match holder. Bellaire Goblet Co. #600, circa late 1880's. Same as Three Dolphin Match without the dolphins. Clear, amber and blue. Some attribute earlier production to Bryce Bros. at Pittsburgh, Pa. Shards of Stars & Bars pattern were found at Bellaire site in Findlay, Ohio. Ref: H-1 #364.

350. BEARDED MAN WITH STAFF aka MAN WITH PACK ON BACK. Clear found marked "Portieux." Variants lack barrel by man and have different weave on basket. Known in clear, clear with frosted and amber. Ref: M-TP, plate xxx.

351. COOLIE (NBK). Marked with an "S" and a "V" in different locations. Probably French. Age unknown.

352. HAND WITH FAN. Match holder. Probably early 20th century. White and blue milk glass, both decorated and undecorated. Maker unknown.

353. PEEK-A-BOO aka CHERUBS. McKee Glass Co., circa 1910-1920. This one believed to be old, but several newer ones known with variations on top rim and base. Ref: H-1000 #734-735.

354. DOG WITH HAT. Belmont Glass Co. of Bellaire, Ohio, circa 1885. Reproduced in many colors. Original colors of clear, amber, vaseline and blue. May be frosted. Ref: H-1000 #333.

355. FLEUR DE LIS. Challinor & Taylor, then by U.S. Glass Co., circa late 1800's. Made in clear, white milk, blue milk and rare in ruby stain. Sometimes decorated with flowers. Ref: H-1000 #853.

356. BEGGARS HAND. Found labeled Portieux, Vallerysthal, France. Old are circa 1900. Clear, frosted, and opaque colors of white, blue and green. A clear one with distinct scallops, but almost no pebble on base effect may be of recent origin. Ref: H-1000 #370.

357. TREE OF LIFE. Portland Glass, circa 1870. Heacock questioned whether this apple green or the light amber were made in the 1867-1873 time frame and if this is a toothpick holder or an egg cup. Also made in sapphire blue and vaseline. Ref: H-1000 #197.

358. BABY MINE aka FANCY ELEPHANT. Enterprise Manufacturing Co. of Akron, Ohio. Clear, clear frosted, cobalt blue, bright blue, amber, milk and green. Ref: H-CG #2.

359. STOVE. Pattern named after the old pot bellied stoves. This is a rare salt shaker that has been ground down. Ref: P-GSS #40Q.

360. SKOOKUMS. Marked "George Borgfeld & Co. sole licensees, J.S. Sears. 1916. U.S.Des.Pat." Candy container or bank. The twist-on lid was slotted so SKOOKUMS could be used as a bank when the candy was gone. Ref: EA-CC.

361. WITCH HEAD aka OLD WOMAN. Indiana Tumbler & Goblet Co. of Greentown, Indiana, circa 1894-1903. Known in clear, nile green, and chocolate. Widely reproduced for many years including an almost nile green color, chocolate, and cobalt blue iridized. Old ones are rarely found. Ref: M-GG.

362. UPRIGHT PIANO. No information found.

363. BEAD RIM BASKET (NBW). Basket is a yellowish green custard. Does not fluoresce under blacklight. Age and maker unknown.

364. HAT. Cobalt blue. Hats like this were often fashioned from tumbler molds. Maker unknown.

365. DAWN TO DUSK HAT (Name by Phillips). 1918-1920 by an unknown glass blower, who produced small vases for the Clarence & John Dettling florist business in Akron, Ohio. The blower had previously worked for LaBelle Glass Co. From his home near Bellaire, Ohio, he blew glass decorated with "Rainbow Lustres" in six different shapes for the floral business. (This information is taken from a story that first appeared in a Carnival glass club newsletter in August, 1966.)

366. POLKA DOT (OMN). Blown hat. George Duncan Co., circa 1884-1890. The pattern is known generically as Inverted Thumbprint. Ref: BFM-DUN.

367. MODERN HAT. Rim is ribbed. Row of stars around the base. Alternating vertical panels, one with stippling and the next an English hobnail type. Possibly circa 1970's.

368. AURORA JEWELS. Imperial Glass Co., 1950's-1980's. Often found in this carnival cobalt color. Heisey hats from the same mold are occasionally found in clear and are unmarked. Made as a match or cigarette holder.

369. BLOWN HAT. Peachblow made by Pairpoint, New Bedford, Mass. in the late 1980's.

370. TAPERED BLOCK HAT. Made by Kemple in the 1950's-1960's. Clear, vaseline, light blue and bluish green. Ref: H-1000 #199.

371. DAISY & BUTTON HAT. Fenton, circa 1960's-1970's. Marked inside with an "O V G" logo. Olde Virginia Glass is a Fenton trademark. Made in blue, custard, carnival, milk and other colors.

372. RAINDROP HAT NO. 1 (NBW). Brim has parallel rows of 29 raindrops. Body has optic diamond pattern. Known in amber, blue, emerald green and canary. Clear not listed by Lee. (RAINDROP HAT NO. 2 (NBW) has two staggered rows of 13 raindrops each on the brim. Body has exterior hob pattern in rows that angle. Hat band has bow and may say "Pat. applied for." Number designations were added to names to eliminate confusion of duplicate names found in Lee's reference. Known in amber, blue, apple green and canary according to Lee. Both circa 1880's. Ref: H-R/U #1329 and L-VG plate 157 (#1) and plate 159 (#2).

373. MILLEFIORE HAT. Believed to be circa 1980's from Murano, Italy.

374. BLOWN HAT. Optic ribs. Craquelle glass with a smooth rim. Maker and age unknown.

375. SPATTER HAT. Uncased spatter. Maker unknown. Possibly Czech origin.

376. DAISY & BUTTON HAT. Fenton. Made for many years, this is probably recent.

377. BRISTOL TYPE HAT. Bluish white color, circa 1890's. Probably English. Ref: L-VG plate 131.

378. HAT. Fenton hobnail in topaz opalescent. Circa 1950-1980's. Made in other Fenton colors.

379. HAT. Opaque glass with pink lining. Probably Sagamore Glass (formerly Pairpoint/Bryden) of recent vintage.

380. SPIRIT OF '76. Made for 1976 NTHCS convention (the first) at Cambridge, Ohio by Mosser Glass Co. of that city. Made in iridized and non-iridized cobalt blue. The bottom reads "T.H.C.S.-1976" ("National" was not a part of the Society's name at this time) in an outside ring and "R.W." (for Robert Wetzel, the mold maker) over a line and "J.K." (for Judy Knauer, designer of the toothpick holder and Founder of NTHCS) below a line across the center. In honor of our country's bicentennial, the design featured a frond with 13 parts representing the original 13 colonies, a likeness of the Liberty Torch and a bracket motif that when inverted represented "76." Successive issues of this toothpick holder were made in red and white.

381. SPIRIT OF '76. Made by Mosser Glass Co. of Cambridge, Ohio for 1977 NTHCS convention at Dearborn, Michigan. Made in iridized and non-iridized red. The bottom reads "DEARBORN, MI" and "NTHCS" in an outside ring and "AUG. 1977" in the center. Also see information on #380.

382. SPIRIT OF '76. Made by Mosser Glass Co. of Cambridge, Ohio for 1978 NTHCS convention at St. Louis, Missouri. Made in iridized and non-iridized white (milk) glass. The bottom reads "N.T.H.C.S." and "ST. LOUIS, MO." in an outside ring and "AUG 1978" in the center. Also see information on #380.

383. NOUVEAU ART. Hand blown by Joe Hamon, Colorado, and hand decorated by Rueven in a style known as "Israeli Original" for the 1979 NTHCS convention at West Chester, Pa.

384. TEXAS ROSE. Hand painted china by Carolyn Oman of Republic, Mo. for the 1980 NTHCS convention held at Irving, Texas. Only 100 were made.

Note: Fearing that there would be no convention toothpick holder, Wm. (Bill) Heacock arranged for a supply of Fenton Art Glass Co. No. 8294, PANELLED DAISY, holders in the color cameo opalescent. These were given as souvenirs at the convention banquet. These holders (not pictured here) are regular production items and are unmarked. PANELLED DAISY aka BRAZIL is a pattern originally produced by U.S. Glass Co., but no original toothpick holder is known. This pedestalled item was sold both as a toothpick holder and a candle holder in the 1980's in blue, lime green, cobalt carnival and other Fenton colors.

385. GALLOWAY aka VIRGINIA. Made by Mosser Glass Co. of Cambridge, Ohio for the 1981 NTHCS convention held in Dayton, Ohio. It is a copy of an old U.S. Glass Co. pattern, and was marked "N.T.H.C.S.", "DAYTON, OH", and "1981" on the bottom.

386. ILLINOIS GOLD (NBW). Hand blown and iridized by Terry Crider of Wapakoneta, Ohio for the 1982 NTHCS convention at Rock Island, Illinois. It is hand signed on the bottom with "N.T.H.C.S., 1982, ILLINOIS, CRIDER".

387. PAINTED POST. Made for the 1983 NTHCS convention in Painted Post, New York by Vitrix, a studio in Corning, N.Y. The bottom is inscribed "Vitrix, NTHCS, 1983".

388. THREADS OF GOLD. Hand blown and iridized by Terry Crider in his studio at Wapakoneta, Ohio for the 1984 NTHCS convention at St. Louis, Mo. The bottom is inscribed "N.T.H.C.S., 1984" and signed "Crider".

389. CHERRY THUMBPRINTS. Made by Mosser Glass Co. of Cambridge, Ohio for the 1985 NTHCS convention at Cambridge, Ohio. This is an old Northwood pattern made mostly in crystal and carnival, in which no toothpick holder is known. Mosser also sold these as part of a toy table set in the 1980's. The convention souvenirs have "10th Anniversary, Cambridge, Ohio", painted in gold around the bottom.

390. AMANA. Made by Pilgrim Glass of Ceredo, West Virginia for the 1986 NTHCS convention held at Iowa City, Iowa. The bottom is inscribed or acid stamped only with a faint "1986".

391. PAIRPOINT BUTTERFLY. Made by the Pairpoint Mfg. Co. of New Bedford, Mass. for the 1987 NTHCS convention at New Bedford, Mass. The hat is marked "NTHCS 89" and the Pairpoint logo, "P" in a diamond, is hand painted just under the flower spray on the brim of the hat.

392. GOLDEN WAVES. Hand blown and signed by Joel Bloomberg of California for the 1988 NTHCS convention at Carlsbad, CA.

393. FAIRBORN SWIRL. Hand blown by Boyer Glassworks Studio & Gallery of Harbor Springs, MI, for the 1989 NTHCS convention at Fairborn, Ohio.

394. IOWA BELLE. Hand blown by Terry Crider of Wapakoneta, Ohio for the 1990 NTHCS convention at Dubuque, Iowa. It is signed by Crider.

395. BRENNER-HALL. Hand pressed by Dalzell-Viking in 1991 in a mold which utilized a winning design by NTHCS member Robert Hall, Wilmington, DE. Another member, Peggy Brenner, by remembering the Society in her will, provided the funds to complete this project which was begun in 1980. NTHCS members previewed this holder at the 1991 convention in Marietta, Ohio and later received them as gifts by mail. They are marked "BRENNER", "HALL", and "NTHCS 1991".

396. ROYAL BAYREUTH. Sunbonnet Babies Ironing. Unmarked. Previously unlisted scene.

397. ROYAL BAYREUTH. Sunbonnet Babies Washing. Blue, green or grey-green "medallion" mark. Unlisted shape.

398. ROYAL BAYREUTH. Sunbonnet Babies Sweeping. Unmarked. Unlisted shape.

399. ROYAL BAYREUTH. People, Woman Gleaning. Marked "Royal Bayreuth P.T. RU 1794, Bavaria". One handle.

400. ROYAL BAYREUTH. Rose Tapestry. Blue mark. Similar to H-1000 #882, but without handles.

401. ROYAL BAYREUTH. Tapestry, Swans. Unmarked.

402. ROYAL BAYREUTH. Tapestry, People. Courting scene. Blue mark. Unlisted scene.

403. ROYAL BAYREUTH. Rose Tapestry. Unmarked. This orange and gold color is more rare than the pink Rose Tapestry, but the workmanship is not as intricate. Unlisted scene.

404. ROYAL BAYREUTH. Animals, Sheep. Unmarked. Other companies made similar shapes. Attribution based on typical animal scene and colors.

405. ROYAL BAYREUTH. Tapestry, Polar Bears. Unmarked. The shape and scene are typical. For shape see H-R/U #1415 and H-1000 #878.

406. ROYAL BAYREUTH. Tapestry, Three Cows and Tree. Unmarked. Unlisted scene. For shape, see H-R/U #1415 and H-1000 #878.

407. ROYAL BAYREUTH. Animals, Bluebirds. Partial mark. Pictures five birds.

408. ROYAL BAYREUTH. Tapestry, scenic. Grotto through the woods. Unmarked. Shape - see #405 above.

409. ROYAL BAYREUTH. Tapestry, Japanese Chrysanthemum. Green mark. New scene. Shape - see #405 above.

410. ROYAL BAYREUTH. Rose Tapestry. Unmarked. Shape - see #405 above.

411. ROYAL BAYREUTH. Tapestry, Castle in the Mountains. Scene unlisted. Unmarked.

412. ROYAL BAYREUTH. Animals, five sheep. Blue mark. Unlisted shape.

413. ROYAL BAYREUTH. People and animals. Farmer and two draft horses with trees and buildings in the background. Blue mark. Unlisted scene.

414. ROYAL BAYREUTH. People and animals. Trainer and two race horses with trees and buildings in the background. Blue mark.

415. ROYAL BAYREUTH. Animals, a penguin. Unmarked. This is an unlisted scene.

416. ROYAL BAYREUTH. People and animals, girl with three geese and mountains in the background. Blue mark. Unlisted scene.

417. ROYAL BAYREUTH. People and animals, Boy sitting on log beside donkey with trees in background. Blue mark. Unlisted scene.

418. ROYAL BAYREUTH. Babes in the woods, boy doffing his hat. Unmarked.

419. ROYAL BAYREUTH. People, two musicians. Blue mark. Unlisted shape and scene.

420. ROYAL BAYREUTH. Children, boy racing girl toward another boy waiting to call the winner, all with wooden shoes. Export numbers "30" and "24" stamped in gold are the only marks.

421. ROYAL BAYREUTH. Children, Beach Babies. Two girls and boy running barefoot on beach with another shore visible in the background. Blue mark. Unlisted scene.

422. ROYAL BAYREUTH. Children, two Dutch boys and a girl jumping rope with windmill in the background. Export number "25" fired in gold is the only mark. Unlisted shape and scene.

423. ROYAL BAYREUTH. Nursery rhymes, Little Miss Muffet jumping up to run away. Blue mark and small shield with "B T" and crown over the top and "Germany" underneath.

424. ROYAL BAYREUTH. Children, girl walking a dog with trees and house in background. Blue mark. Unlisted shape and scene.

425. ROYAL BAYREUTH. Nursery rhymes, Little Bo-Peep with woods in the background. Unmarked. Unlisted shape and scene.

426. ROYAL BAYREUTH. Nursery rhymes, Jack & Jill. Blue mark. Unlisted shape and scene.

427. ROYAL BAYREUTH. Nursery rhymes, Jack & Jill with a well in the background and pail at Jack's feet. Blue mark and small shield with "B.T." and crown over the top, "Germany" underneath. Unlisted scene.

428. R.S. PRUSSIA. Red mark. Mold No. 268 (Iris mold) Ref: G-RS2 page 114 #318.

429. R.S. PRUSSIA. Red mark. Probably mold No. 631 (Medallion mold). Ref: G-RS2 page 115, #325.

430. R.S. PRUSSIA. Red mark. Mold No. 526 (Carnation mold). Ref: G-RS2 page 97, #256. See #435 below.

431. R.S. PRUSSIA. Red mark.

432. R.S. PRUSSIA. Red mark.

433. R.S. PRUSSIA. Red mark. Mold No. 501 (Surreal Dogwood Blossoms). Ref: G-RSl page 123, #297.

434. R.S. PRUSSIA. Red mark.

435. R.S. PRUSSIA. Red mark. See #430 above.

436. R.S. PRUSSIA. Red mark. Mold # 627. Ref: G-RSl page 145, #375.

437. R.S. PRUSSIA. Red mark.

438. R.S. PRUSSIA. Red mark. Mold #644 (Poppies). Ref: G-RS2 page 119, #342.

439. R.S. PRUSSIA TYPE. Unmarked. The Three Swans is the most famous R.S. Prussia scene.

440. R.S. PRUSSIA TYPE. Maker and date unknown.

441. R.S. PRUSSIA. Star mark.

442. R.S. PRUSSIA TYPE. No mark.

443. R.S. PRUSSIA TYPE. No mark.

444. R.S. GERMANY. Marked.

445. R.S. GERMANY. Green star mark.

446. R.S. GERMANY. Green mark. Artist signed, possibly "Veazel." Ref: G-RSl page 36 mark No. 27.

447. R.S. TILLOWITZ. Silesia. Marked. Ref: G-RSl page 36 mark No. 30.

448. R.S. GERMANY. Red mark.

449. R.S. GERMANY. Green mark. Hand painted.

450. R.S. GERMANY. Green mark. Ref: G-RSl page 36 mark No. 27.

451. R.S. GERMANY. Blue mark. Artist signed. Ref: G-RSl page 35 mark No. 25.

452. R.S. GERMANY. Marked. Ref: G-RSl page 35 mark No. 25.

453. R.S. GERMANY TYPE. No mark.

454. R.S. GERMANY TYPE. No mark.

455. R.S. GERMANY. Green mark.

456. R.S. GERMANY. Green mark. Ref: G-RSl page 35 mark No. 26.

457. R.S. GERMANY. Green mark.

458. E.S. GERMANY. Portrait china. Visible portion of mark reads "PROV SAXE E S Germany." Ref: K-NDM #35P.

459. R.S. GERMANY. Marked. Also see #558.

460. NIPPON. Marked with a green M in a wreath.

461. NIPPON. Not marked. Tentative identification.

462. NIPPON. 2" tall, 1 1/2" opening. Marked "Hand Painted Nippon." Ref: V-NIP #80.

463. NIPPON. Marked with blue rising sun mark.

464. NIPPON. Marked with blue rising sun mark.

465. NIPPON. Marked with blue M in a wreath. Ref: V-NIP 1 mark # 47 and V-NIP 2 #1199.

466. NIPPON. Marked "Hand Painted Nippon" with M in a wreath.

467. NIPPON. Marked "Hand Painted" with a green seal M. Nippon.

468. NIPPON. Marked "Hand Painted Nippon".

469. NIPPON. Marked. 2 1/2" high, 1 3/4" wide.

470. NIPPON. Not marked.

471. NORITAKE. Swan on Lake. Marked "Japan". Six sided.

472. CHINA. Phoenix Bird pattern. Marked "Japan".

473. MAJOLICA. Made in England, but not marked. References include an article in September 1982 NTHCS *Toothpick Bulletin* and an article from *Woman's Day* magazine from 1967.

474. NIPPON. Moriage type of decoration. Very thin. Blue leaf "Nippon" and "Hand Painted" marks.

475. CHINA. Unmarked.

476. NIPPON. Marked with green M.

477. NIPPON. Marked with green M in a wreath and "Nippon, Hand Painted".

478. NIPPON. Marked with M and "Hand Painted Nippon".

479. NIPPON. Marked with M in a green wreath. 2" tall.

480. NIPPON. Marked with blue rising sun. Ref: V-NIP 1 #84.

481. NIPPON. Marked with M in green wreath. Hand Painted. Ref: V-NIP 3 #47 and V-NIP 3 plate 2145.

482. NIPPON. Matte finish. Marked "Hand Painted Nippon" and M in a wreath.

483. NIPPON. Marked "Hand Painted Nippon" and M in a wreath. 2 3/4" high.

484. CHINA. No marks. Believed to be Japanese.

485. NIPPON. Marked "Hand Painted Nippon" with M in a wreath. Pattern is "Palms and Lakes." Ref: V-NIP 3 #47.

486. NIPPON. Marked "Hand Painted Nippon" with a blue rising sun mark.

487. NORITAKE. Green mark. Ref: V-NOR #27 and page 122, plate 113.

488. NIPPON. Marked "Hand Painted Nippon" with green M in a wreath. Believed to be circa 1911.

489. NIPPON. Marked "Imperial Nippon, Hand Painted" with a logo in a circle in blue.

490. NIPPON. Marked "Hand Painted Nippon" with a blue maple leaf. Ref: V-NIP 1 #52 and V-NIP 3 #1203.

491. NIPPON. Marked "Hand Painted Nippon" with blue rising sun. 1 5/8" across top, 2" high.

492. ROYAL DOULTON. Marked "Royal Doulton" in a circle with a crown over "Made in England" and "D5175". The character is Mr. Pickwick.

493. ROYAL DOULTON. Marked "Royal Doulton" in a circle, "England" and "D 2487". The figure is Mr. Micawber.

494. ROYAL DOULTON. "Izaak Walton". No mark indicated.

495. ROYAL DOULTON. Marked "Tony Weller" with crown over Royal Doulton logo and "D5175 and "Made in England".

496. ROYAL DOULTON. "Dr. Johnson, Fleet Street". Marked with shield logo over a banner saying "OLD LONDON" and "ROYAL DOULTON".

497. ROYAL DOULTON. "Tony Weller." Marked with crown logo, "Made in England" and "O 5175".

498. ROYAL DOULTON. Marked "Royal Doulton" with a lion above a crown and "England".

499. ROYAL DOULTON. Figure marked "Orlando" in the picture shown.

500. ROYAL DOULTON. Marked. 2 1/2" high. Sheep in the foreground of this farm scene.

501. ROYAL DOULTON. Printed green mark of lion over crown. "England". Circa 1902 based on mark.

502. ROYAL DOULTON. Marked in circular logo with crown and lion, "Made in England" and "D 5175". The scene is Mr. Micawber.

503. ROYAL DOULTON. Marked in circular logo "England" and "Copyright".

504. ROYAL DOULTON. Marked in circular logo, "Made in England, Sir Roger Coverly, D 5814." The base shows a riding crop and hunting horn.

505. ROYAL DOULTON. Marked.

506. ROYAL DOULTON. Marked with crown logo and "Made in England". This is "Isaac Walton".

507. ROYAL DOULTON. Figure is Mr. Micawber.

508. GOSS. Marked "W.H. Goss". Souvenir of "Stel Fortuna Doraus Harrow".

509. GOSS. Marked "W.H. Goss" with eagle logo.

510. GOSS. Marked. Souvenir of "Cheshire".

511. GOSS. Marked with eagle logo and "Rd #390788" (a 1902 design registry number).

BURMESE GLASS

MT WASHINGTON ART GLASS

ART GLASS

MOLD BLOWN GLASS

63 64 65 66
67 68 69 70
71 72 73 74
75 76 77 78

21

AMBERINA GLASS

CRANBERRY GLASS

ART GLASS

25

141 142 143 144
145 146 147 148 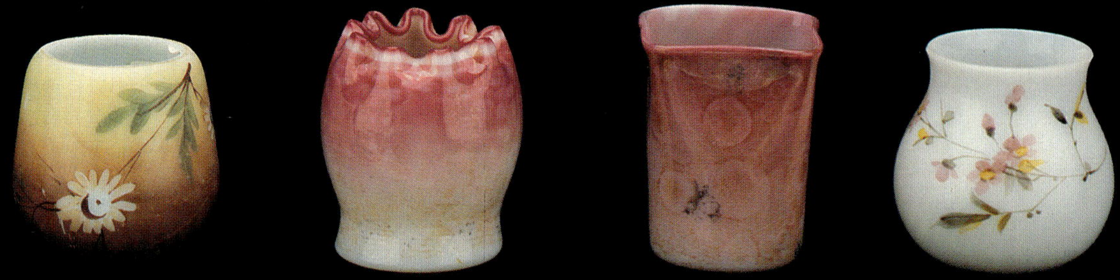
149 150 151 152 
153 154 155 156

26

157  158  159  160

161  162  163  164

165  166  167  168

169 170 171 172

27

IRIDESCENT GLASS

28

CONTEMPORARY ART GLASS

29

ART GLASS

30

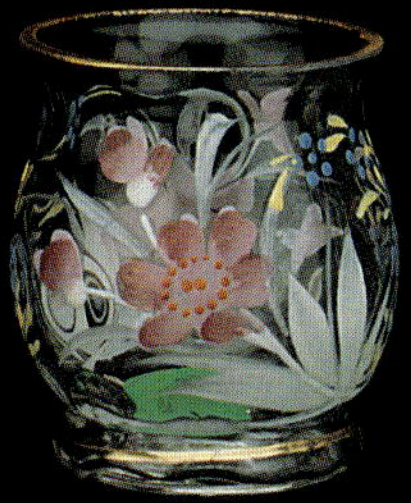

221

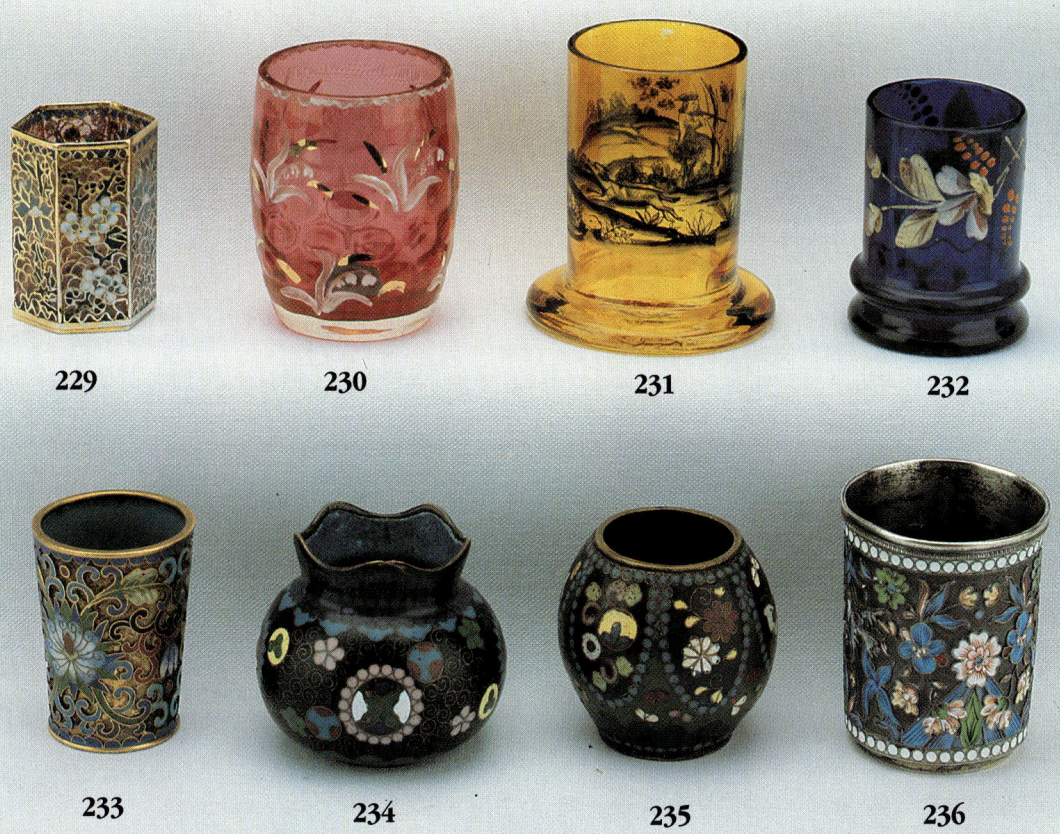

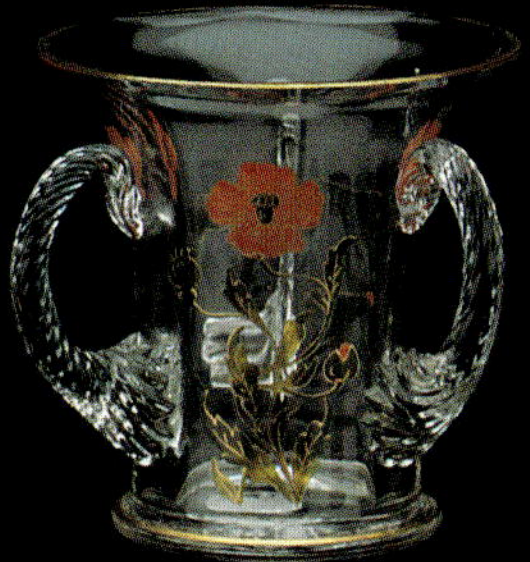

222

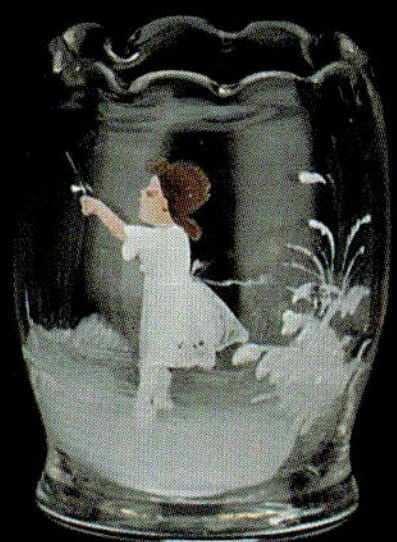

223

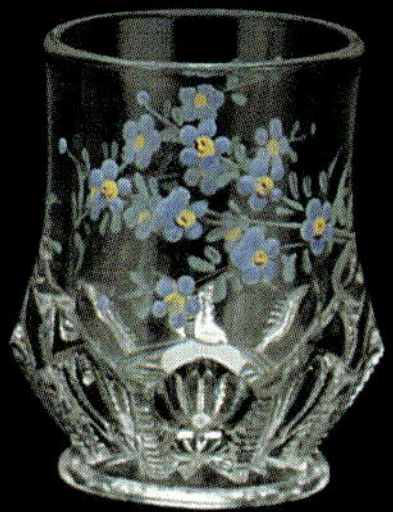

224

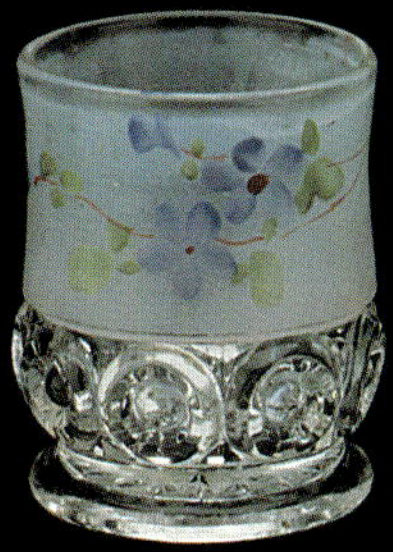

225

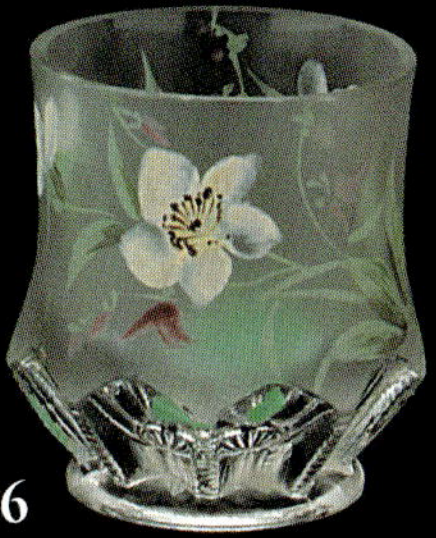

226

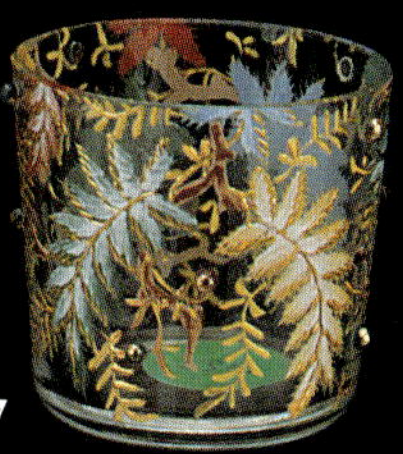

227

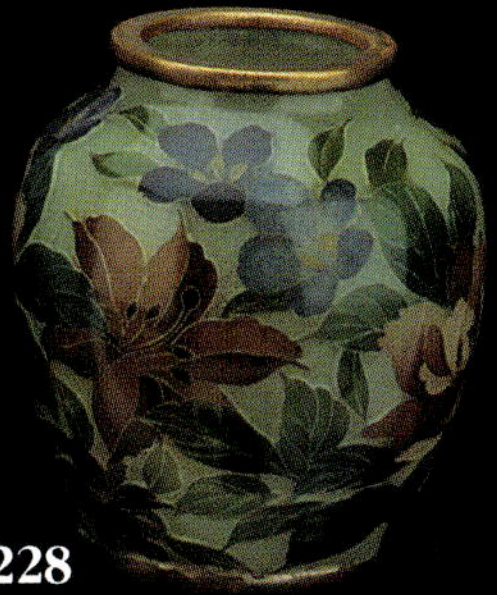

228

229

230

231

232

233

234

235

236

COLORED GLASS

RUBY STAINED GLASS

COLORED GLASS

MISCELLANEOUS GLASS

284 285 286 287

288 289 290 291

292 293 294 295

296 297 298 299

35

MISCELLANEOUS GLASS

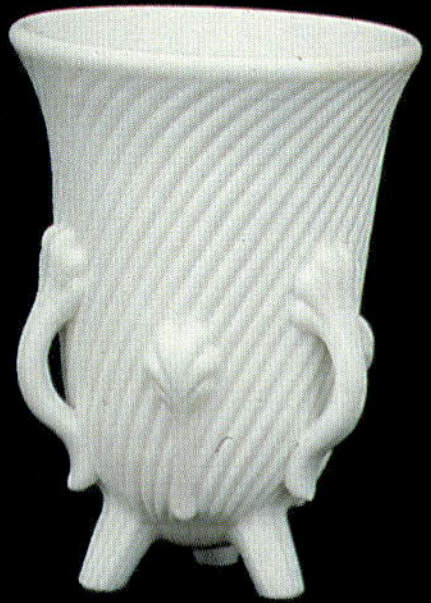

300  301 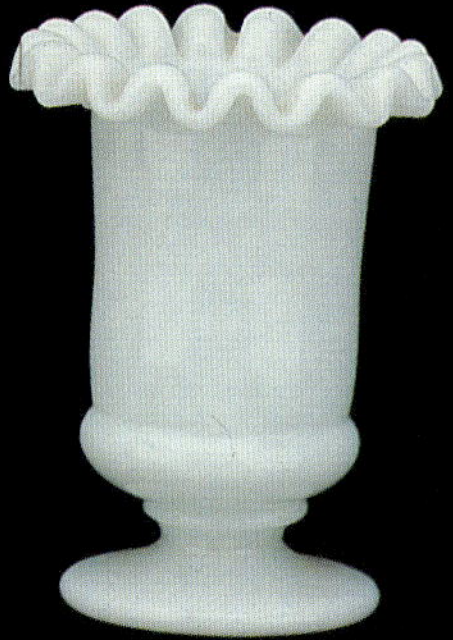 302  303
304  305  306  307 
308  309  310  311 
312 313 314 315

36

ART DECO AND EUROPEAN ART GLASS

316 317 318 319
320 321 322 323
324 325 326 327
328 329 330 331

37

FIGURALS AND MISCELLANEOUS GLASS

GLASS FIGURALS

349 350 351 352
353 354 355 356
357 358 359 360
361 362 363

GLASS HATS

40

NTHCS TOOTHPICK HOLDERS

ROYAL BAYREUTH

ROYAL BAYREUTH

R. S. PRUSSIA

R. S. GERMANY

444　　　445　　　446　　　447

448　　　449　　　450　　　451

452　　　453　　　454　　　455

456　　　457　　　458　　　459

NIPPON

NIPPON AND NIPPON TYPE

47

ROYAL DOULTON

492　　　493　　　494　　　495　　　496

497　　　498　　　499　　　500

501　　　502　　　503　　　504

505　　　506　　　507

48

GOSS AND GOSS TYPE

508 509 510 511

512 513 514 515

516 517 518 519

520 521 522 523

PORCELAIN, CHINA AND MAJOLICA

524　525　526　527
528　529　530　531

532　533　534　535
536　537　538　539

50

PORCELAIN, CHINA AND BISQUE

540 541 542 543 544

545 546 547 548

549 550 551 552

553 554 555 556

51

PORCELAIN AND CHINA

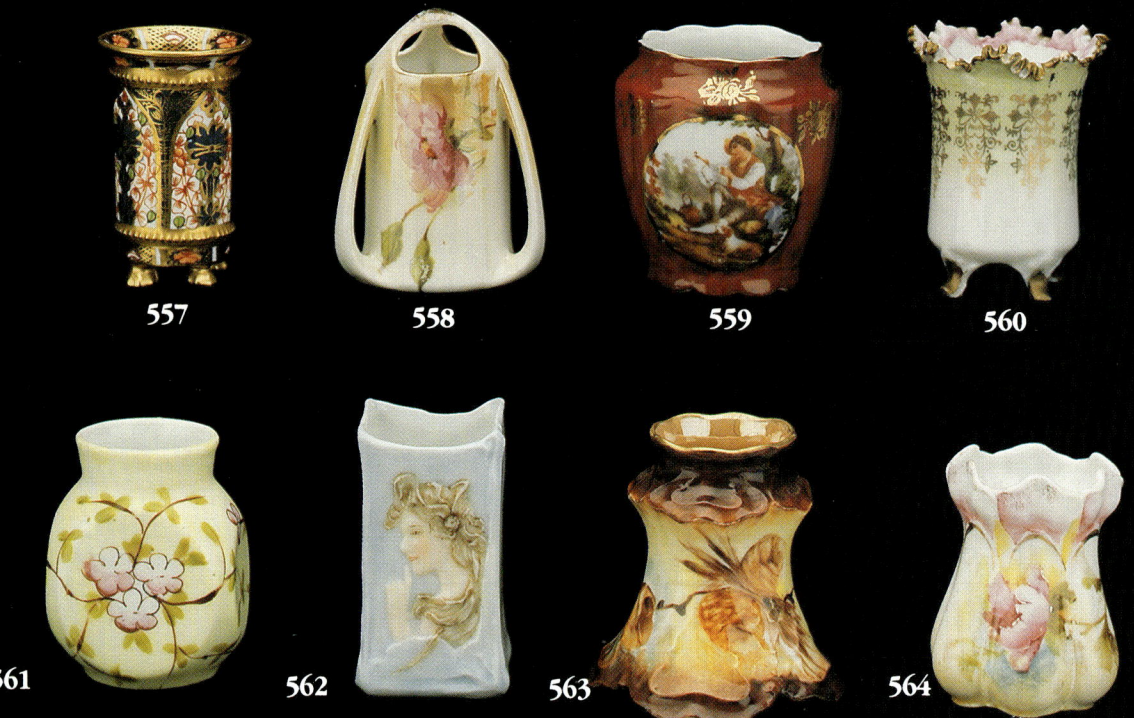

557　558　559　560
561　562　563　564

565　566　567　568
569　570　571　572

EUROPEAN CHINA, PORCELAIN, POTTERY

573 574 575 576

577 578 579 580

581 582 583 584

585 586 587 588

53

CHINA

589 590 591 592

593 594 595 596

597 598 599 600

601 602 603

PORCELAIN AND CHINA

604 605 606 607
608 609 610 611
612 613 614 615
616 617 618 619

55

CHINA, POTTERY AND MISCELLANEOUS

SANITARY TOOTHPICK HOLDERS

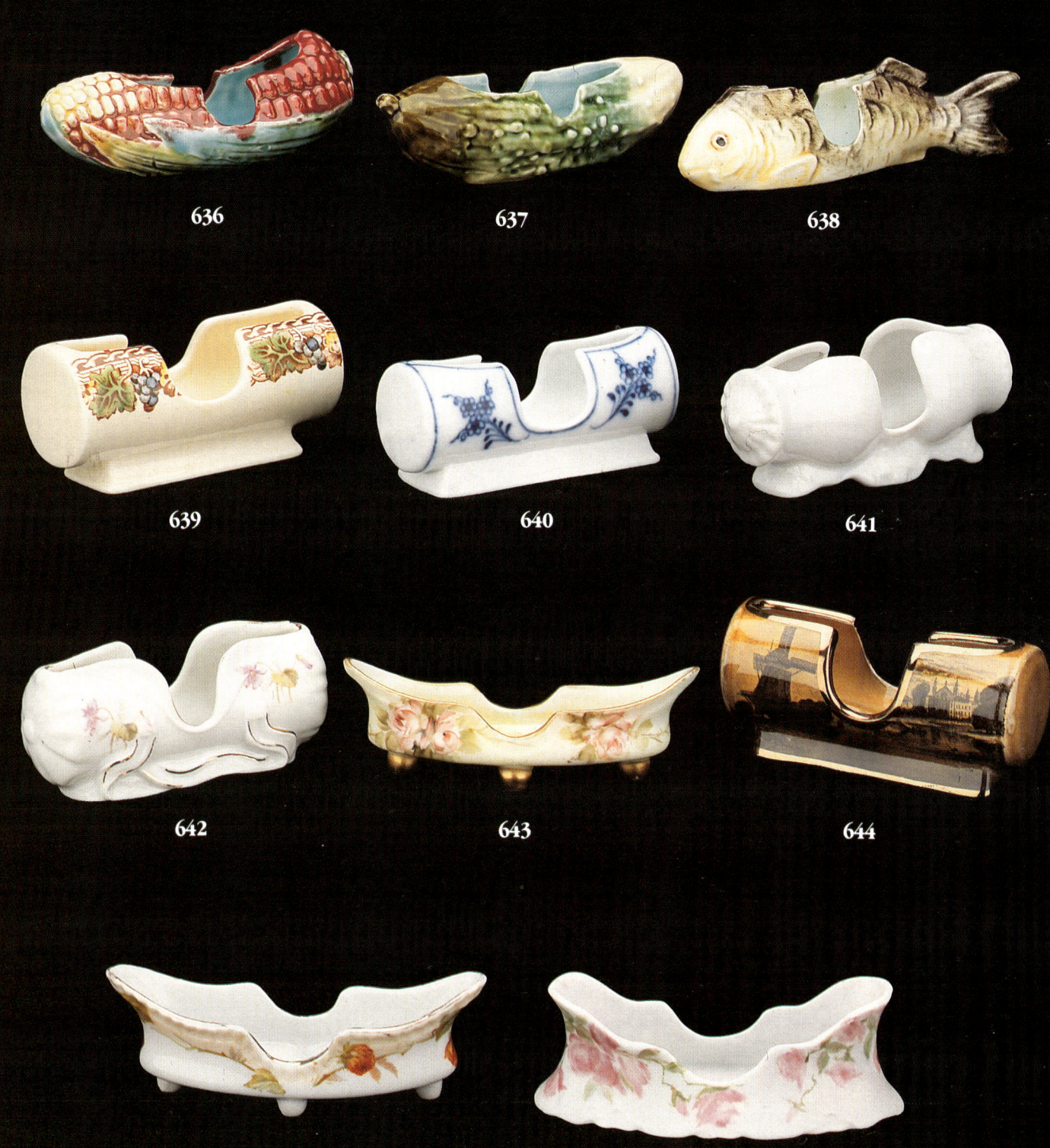

636

637

638

639

640

641

642

643

644

645

646

57

CHINA AND BISQUE FIGURALS

58

BISQUE FIGURALS

CHINA, BISQUE AND MAJOLICA

Our "SURE THING" NEST EGG.

Most natural of all nest eggs. Heavy opal glass. "Firsts." Safely packed. 1 doz. in spaced box. Per dozen, 18c (Case of gross, no pkg. charge, $2.00 gross.)

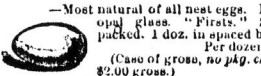

"BEAUTY" MATCH OR TOOTHPICK.

Staple as wheat—5-cent seller.

A dainty little item in pure crystal glass. 1 doz. in box, no charge for package. Per dozen, 28c

5-CENT GLASS HAT.

"Fine as silk"—a nickel seller.

C317—Of the best flint glass made up to illustrate the good old grandfather's hat. For matches, toothpicks, etc. 1 doz. in box. Per dozen, 32c.

COMMON SENSE MATCH SAFE or TOOTHPICK.

One of the things that SELL.

C364—Beaded panel pattern, panels forming numerous scratchers, wide base. 1 doz. in box. Per dozen, 33c.

"DOT MIRROR" TOOTHPICK HOLDER.

New and rich 5-center.

C343—Good size, fancy shape, rich reflecting panel design with fancy foot. 1 doz. in box. Per dozen, 35c.

"RADIANT" TOOTHPICK.

A seller—a bargain.

C352—Good size, richly finished, solid and heavy. Will not tip over easily. Very brilliant. 1 doz. in box. Per dozen, 37c.

"PRISM" TOOTHPICK HOLDER.

Looks like a 10-center.

C360—Ht. 2¼-in., rich cut diamond base, fine flutes and optic bull's eye effect. A full finished beauty. 1 doz. in box. Per dozen, 39c.

GROUND BOTTOM "TUMBLER TOOTHPICK."

Not usually a 5-center.

C346—Ht. 2½-in., extra heavy, figured panel pattern, heavy ground bottom, rich plain edge. Extremely bright and attractive. 1 doz. in box. Per dozen, 39c.

"SIX PANEL" TOOTHPICK HOLDER.

A 5-cent gem.

C347—Of purest crystal, extra heavy and rich panel design, fancy flaring base and scalloped top. 1 doz. in box. Per dozen, 39c.

GYPSY KETTLE.

A 5-cent crystal beauty.

C316—The prettiest and best size kettle made. Very handy for hanging up or for mantel use for matches, picks, etc. 1 doz. in box. Per dozen, 39c.

"RICHEST AND BRIGHTEST" TOOTHPICK HOLDER.

Shapely and attractive.

C341—Purest crystal, beautiful new genuine cut glass pattern, artistic fancy square shape. A 5-cent bargain. 1 doz. in box. Per dozen, 40c

Our "Bon Ton" Toothpick Holder.

Exact reproduction of genuine cut glass. Looks like a 10-center.

C355—Large size, graceful shape, footed, fancy scalloped and flared top, extremely rich and beautiful pattern. Will be an exceptional 5-center. 1 doz. in box. Per dozen, 40c

OUR "BRILLIANT" TOOTHPICK HOLDER.

A bargain at 5 cents or more.

C342—Good size, square shape base, new and rich pattern, having alternating panels in rich cut diamond and plain pattern, with fancy scalloped edge, finished and fire polished. 1 doz. in box. Per dozen, 41c.

OUR "HEAVY CUT" TOOTHPICK HOLDER.

Would be cheap at 10 cents.

C344—Large size, extra heavy, deep, rich cut glass pattern, with heavy plain edge, brilliantly finished and fire polished. 1 doz. in box. Per dozen, 42c.

"LOVING CUP" TOOTHPICK HOLDER.

A dazzling production of best crystal glass.

C353—Imitation cut glass pattern, 3 handles, scalloped top. 1 doz. in box. Per dozen, See vel pp.

"ROSE PINK" TOOTHPICK.

At 10 cents every lady will want one.

C358—Extra heavy cut panel design in rich solid rose pink color, heavy smooth ground and polished bottom. Rich and attractive. 1 doz. in box. Per dozen, 75c

"RUBY AND CRYSTAL" TOOTHPICK.

Rich and brilliant. A pleasing 10-center.

C348—Graceful flaring shape, rich genuine cut pattern with fancy scalloped edge, finished and panels decorated in pure burnt-in ruby. 1 doz. in box. Per dozen, 78c.

"DAINTY" GOLD BAND TOOTHPICK HOLDER.

A little 10-cent gem.

C359—Not large but very beautiful. Rich cut diamond pattern, fancy scalloped edge, 1 wide and 2 narrow gold bands. Will sell if shown. 1 doz. in box. Per dozen, 79c.

"ROSE RED" TOOTHPICK

—With Gold Edges.

At 10 cents will sell always.

C374—Medium size, footed, fancy shape, deep cut panel design in imitation of genuine cut glass, solid burnt-in rose red color with rich band, gold edge. An unusually rich piece. 1 doz. in box, no charge. Per dozen, 82c.

Butler Brothers catalog (1907).

GERMAN CHINA DECORATED TOOTHPICK OR MATCH HOLDER.

Beautiful goods at popular prices. Can be used also as little vases to put in cabinet.

R845, 74c Doz.   R2669, 79c Doz.   R846, 88c Doz.

R845—Vase toothpick. Ht. about 2½-in., 6 styles assorted, solid cobalt blue glazed outside with gold top, attractive floral decorated center in tints and gold. 1 doz. in spaced box ... 74

R2669—Glazed vase assortment. As above, different decorations, half with cobalt blue glazed bodies and half in rich green, watteau group picture fronts with gold work all around in profusion, gold tops. 1 doz. in spaced box, assorted ... 79

R846—Basket catch-all. Good china, ht. (including handles) 2½-in., two open handles, cobalt blue luster body with elaborate floral decorated front in gold and colors, gold edges. 1 doz. in spaced box ... 88

IMPORTED DECORATED CHINA MATCH STAND.

R2585 + Transparent, hexagon shape, clouded gold top, 2 corrugated match scratcher panels, floral spray decorations. Ht. 2½-in. 1 doz. in pkg. ... 44

DECORATED CHINA TOOTHPICK HOLDERS.

Can also be used for match safes or catch-alls.

R513, 31c Doz. R518. R520, 68c Doz. R521, 72c Doz.

R513—"Mikado Pattern." Cylinder shape, dresden blue, underglazed decorations, filled gold band top and bottom, inner delft blue band. 1 doz. in pkg ... $0.31

R518—Panel shape, swell body, embossed, gold top, footed effect, decorations in cluster of flowers. 1 doz. in pkg ... 39

R520—"Kettle Design." Transparent china, good size, flaring top with 2¼-in. opening, gold decorated, decorations in shaded tints, with words "Take your pick" in gold. 1 doz. in pkg ... 68

R521—Fancy shape, gold sponged top, half tinted, luster clouded front with decoration of gold and colored foliage with enameled gold stems, etc. Fine china. 1 doz. in pkg ... 72

R522, 75c Doz.

R522—"Rich Luster." Extra fine china, flaring top with gold band, floral embossed pattern, 4 feet, luster tinted body, gold foliage and flowers ... 75

R2365, 85c Doz.

R2365 + Transparent china, good size, wreath design, embossing, 2 gold showered edge with gold clouds, portrait head decoration with floral headdress. Assorted subjects. 1 doz. in pkg ... 85

R524, 87c Doz.

R524—"Loving Cup." Dainty china, fancy mold, 3 gold showered open handles, gold showered top, decorations in delicate tints with floral sprays strewn all around. Assorted tints. 1 doz. in pkg ... 87

China items from a Butler Brothers catalog (1903).

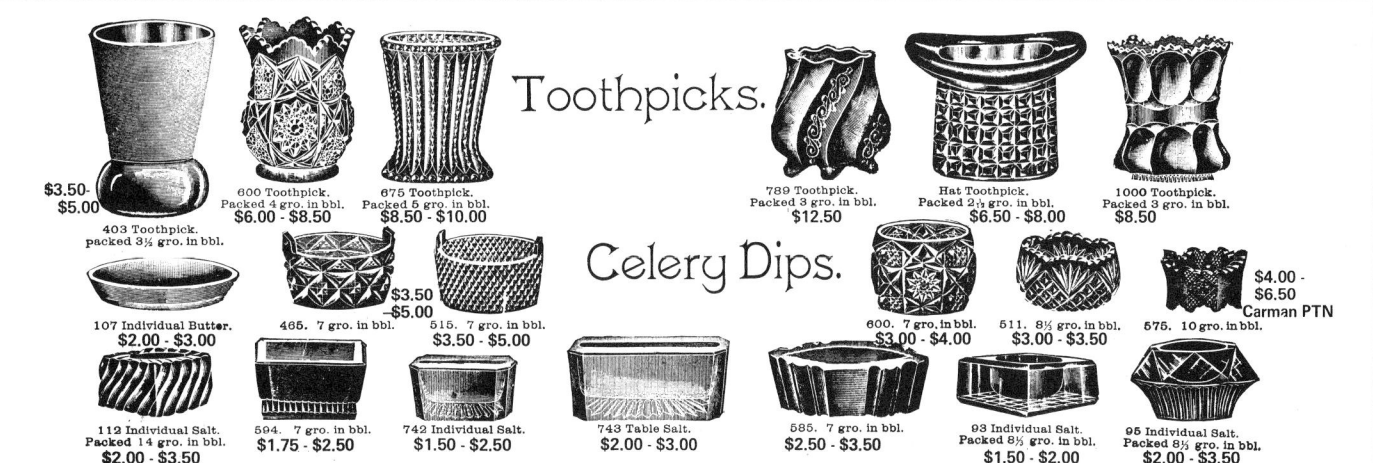

Toothpick holders and individual salts (called "celery dips") from the 1901 catalog of the Fostoria Glass Company of Moundsville, West Virginia.

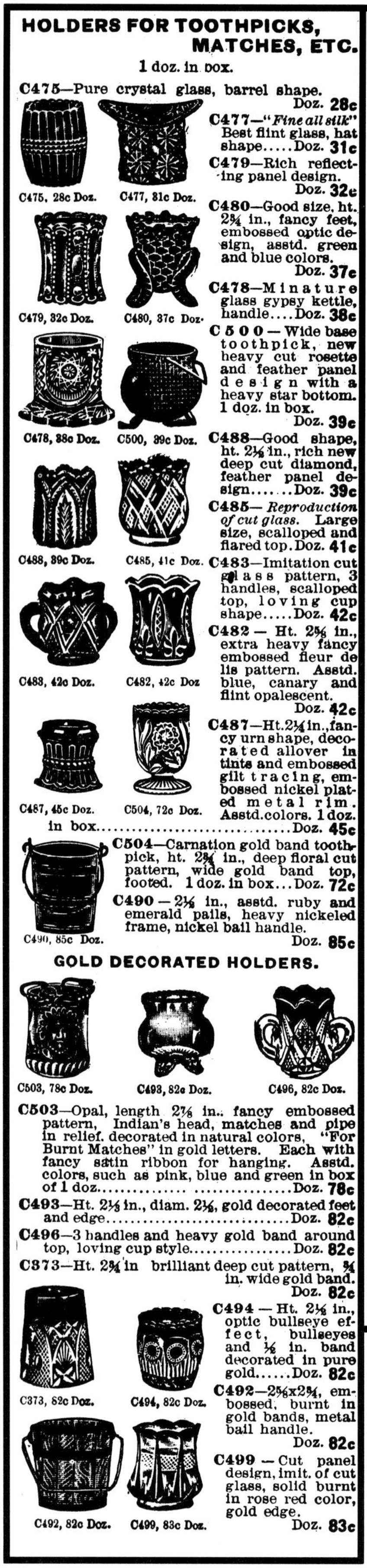

HOLDERS FOR TOOTHPICKS, MATCHES, ETC.

1 doz. in box.

C475—Pure crystal glass, barrel shape. Doz. 28c

C477—"*Fine all silk*" Best flint glass, hat shape.....Doz. 31c

C479—Rich reflecting panel design. Doz. 32c

C480—Good size, ht. 2¾ in., fancy feet, embossed optic design, asstd. green and blue colors. Doz. 37c

C478—Minature glass gypsy kettle, handle....Doz. 38c

C500—Wide base toothpick, new heavy cut rosette and feather panel design with a heavy star bottom. 1 doz. in box. Doz. 39c

C488—Good shape, ht. 2⅛ in., rich new deep cut diamond, feather panel design.......Doz. 39c

C485—*Reproduction of cut glass.* Large size, scalloped and flared top. Doz. 41c

C483—Imitation cut glass pattern, 3 handles, scalloped top, loving cup shape.....Doz. 42c

C482—Ht. 2⅝ in., extra heavy fancy embossed fleur de lis pattern. Asstd. blue, canary and flint opalescent. Doz. 42c

C487—Ht. 2¼ in., fancy urn shape, decorated allover in tints and embossed gilt tracing, embossed nickel plated metal rim. Asstd. colors. 1 doz. in box...............................Doz. 45c

C504—Carnation gold band toothpick, ht. 2¾ in., deep floral cut pattern, wide gold band top, footed. 1 doz. in box...Doz. 72c

C490—2⅛ in., asstd. ruby and emerald pails, heavy nickeled frame, nickel bail handle. Doz. 85c

C475, 28c Doz. C477, 31c Doz. C479, 32c Doz. C480, 37c Doz. C478, 38c Doz. C500, 39c Doz. C488, 39c Doz. C485, 41c Doz. C483, 42c Doz. C482, 42c Doz. C487, 45c Doz. C504, 72c Doz. C490, 85c Doz.

GOLD DECORATED HOLDERS.

C503, 78c Doz. C493, 82c Doz. C496, 82c Doz.

C503—Opal, length 2⅞ in., fancy embossed pattern, Indian's head, matches and pipe in relief, decorated in natural colors, "For Burnt Matches" in gold letters. Each with fancy satin ribbon for hanging. Asstd. colors, such as pink, blue and green in box of 1 doz...............................Doz. 78c

C493—Ht. 2⅓ in., diam. 2⅙, gold decorated feet and edge...............................Doz. 82c

C496—3 handles and heavy gold band around top, loving cup style................Doz. 82c

C373—Ht. 2¾ in brilliant deep cut pattern, ¾ in. wide gold band. Doz. 82c

C494—Ht. 2⅛ in., optic bullseye effect, bullseyes and ½ in. band decorated in pure gold......Doz. 82c

C492—2⅝x2¾, embossed, burnt in gold bands, metal bail handle. Doz. 82c

C499—Cut panel design, imit. of cut glass, solid burnt in rose red color, gold edge. Doz. 83c

C373, 82c Doz. C494, 82c Doz. C492, 82c Doz. C499, 83c Doz.

Butler Brothers catalog (1907).

HOLDERS FOR TOOTHPICKS, MATCHES, ETC.

1 doz. in box.

C500, C501, 31c Doz C502, 33c Doz. C503, 37c Doz.

C500—Pure crystal glass, barrel shape. Temp-Out

C501—"*Fine as silk*" Best flint glass, hat shape. Doz. 31c

C502—Rich reflecting panel design...Doz. 33c

C503—Good size, ht. 2¾ in., fancy feet, embossed optic design, asstd. green and blue colors...............................Doz. 37c

C504—Miniature glass gypsy kettle, handle. Doz. 38c

C505—Wide base toothpick, new heavy cut rosette and feather panel design with a heavy star bottom......Doz. 40c

C485—*Reproduction of cut glass.* Large size, scalloped and flared top. Dz. 41c

C508—Imitation cut glass pattern, 3 handles, scalloped top, loving cup shape....Doz. 42c

C504, 38c Doz. C505, 40c Doz. C485, 41c Doz. C508, 42c Doz

C512—*Easily worth a dime.* Ht. 3½ in., footed fancy urn shape, thin brilliant crystal, fancy double handles. Per dozen, 43c

C512, 43c Doz. C507, 44c Doz.

C507—Ht. 2¾ in., extra heavy pure crystal, wide colonial flute, scalloped edge, star pattern, brilliantly full finished........Doz. 44c

522—Ht. 3 in., heavily embossed, asstd. ruby, green and purple colorings, profuse gold bronze and bright colored decorations, asstd. Doz. 45c

C521—Ht. 2¼ in., fancy shape, asstd. ruby, green and purple, decorated embossed work in colors and gold bronze embossed nickel plated metal rim....................Doz. 47c

C522, 45c Doz. C521, 47c Dz.

HORSESHOE DECORATED TOOTHPICK HOLDER.

Will be a record breaking seller if offered at 5c.

C520—Square shape, footed, ht. 2¼ in. heavy crystal, decorated in allover solid colors, embossed horseshoe and clover leaf on each side in colors and gold bronze. Asstd. ruby, green and purple, in box of 1 doz. Per dozen, 42c

AUTO MATCH OR TOOTHPICK NOVELTY.

C28—Best crystal glass, full finished. 4¾ x 2⅛. 1 doz. in carton......Doz. 82c

Butler Brothers catalog (1906).

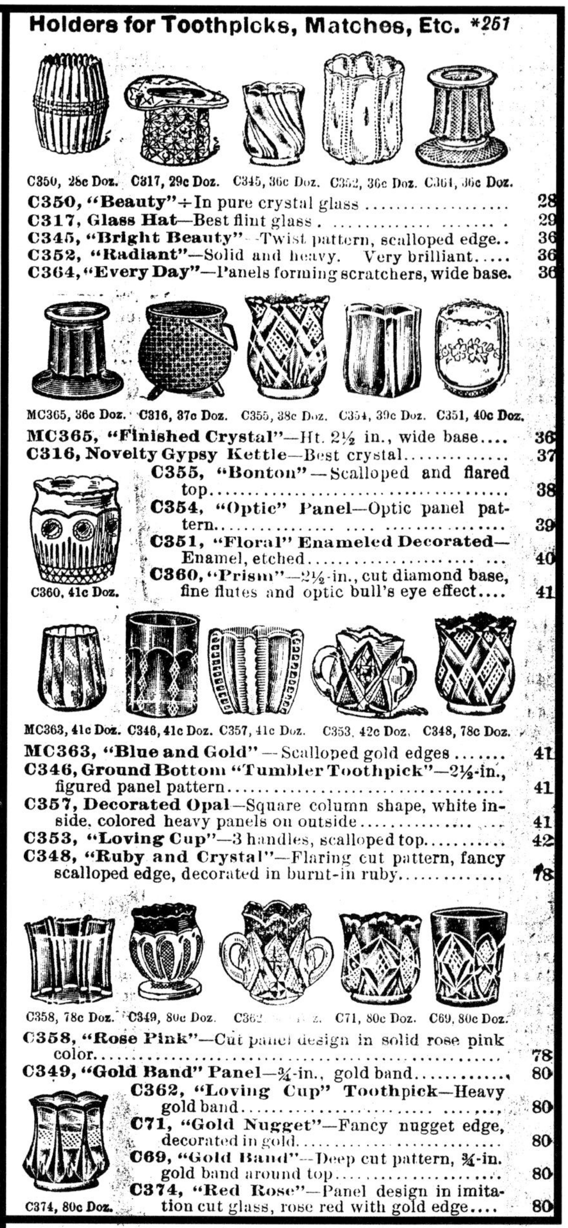

Holders for Toothpicks, Matches, Etc. *251

C350, 28c Doz. C317, 29c Doz. C345, 36c Doz. C352, 36c Doz. C364, 36c Doz.

C350, "Beauty"—In pure crystal glass 28

C317, Glass Hat—Best flint glass 29

C345, "Bright Beauty"—Twist pattern, scalloped edge.. 36

C352, "Radiant"—Solid and heavy. Very brilliant..... 36

C364, "Every Day"—Panels forming scratchers, wide base. 36

MC365, 36c Doz. C316, 37c Doz. C355, 38c Doz. C354, 39c Doz. C351, 40c Doz.

MC365, "Finished Crystal"—Ht. 2½ in., wide base.... 36

C316, Novelty Gypsy Kettle—Best crystal............ 37

C355, "Bonton"—Scalloped and flared top.............................. 38

C354, "Optic" Panel—Optic panel pattern.............................. 39

C351, "Floral" Enameled Decorated—Enamel, etched.............................. 40

C360, "Prism"—2½-in., cut diamond base, fine flutes and optic bull's eye effect.... 41

C360, 41c Doz.

MC363, 41c Doz. C346, 41c Doz. C357, 41c Doz. C353, 42c Doz. C348, 78c Doz.

MC363, "Blue and Gold"—Scalloped gold edges 41

C346, Ground Bottom "Tumbler Toothpick"—2½-in., figured panel pattern.............................. 41

C357, Decorated Opal—Square column shape, white inside, colored heavy panels on outside.............. 41

C353, "Loving Cup"—3 handles, scalloped top.......... 42

C348, "Ruby and Crystal"—Flaring cut pattern, fancy scalloped edge, decorated in burnt-in ruby............. 78

C358, 78c Doz. C349, 80c Doz. C362 ... C71, 80c Doz. C69, 80c Doz.

C358, "Rose Pink"—Cut panel design in solid rose pink color.............................. 78

C349, "Gold Band" Panel—¾-in., gold band............ 80

C362, "Loving Cup" Toothpick—Heavy gold band.............................. 80

C71, "Gold Nugget"—Fancy nugget edge, decorated in gold.............................. 80

C69, "Gold Band"—Deep cut pattern, ¾-in. gold band around top.............................. 80

C374, "Red Rose"—Panel design in imitation cut glass, rose red with gold edge.... 80

C374, 80c Doz.

Butler Brothers catalog (1902).

ALUMINUM SETS.

T1358 T1343

T1358, 4 Pc. Table Set—4⅞x3⅜ satin finish tray, embossed polished edge, loaded bottom, polished top salt and pepper shakers, loaded bottom, satin finish toothpick holder. 1 set in box.....................Doz. sets, $2.10

T1343, Sugar and Cream Set—Satin finish, 5¼ in. tray, polished rim, 2¼ in. creamer, polished top, bottom and riveted handle, 2¾ in. sugar, polished top. 1 set in box..Set, 33c

SELF RIGHTING TOOTHPICK HOLDERS.

T1355—*10 cent seller & money maker.* 1¾x1¾, asstd. new cut diamond and swell pattern, satin finish inside and out, polished loaded bottoms. 1 doz. in box, asstd. Doz. 69c

MATCH HOLDER AND ASH TRAY.

T333—4¼x1⅙, satin finish, cup 1½x1¾, large tray. Each wrapped. 1 doz. in box. Doz. 87c

Butler Brothers catalog (1911).

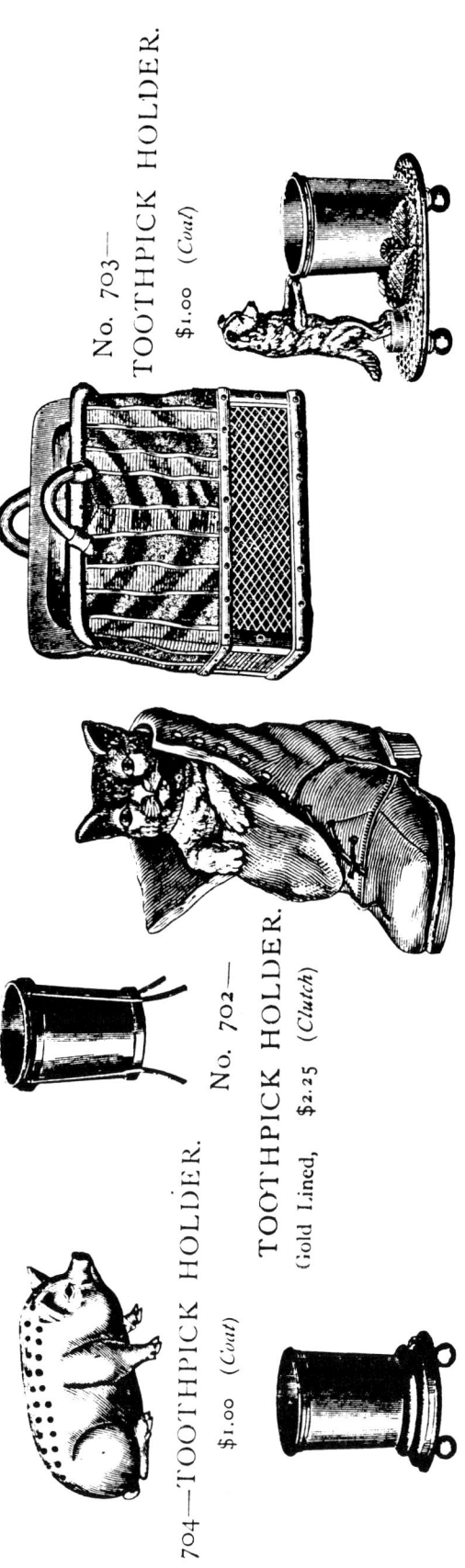

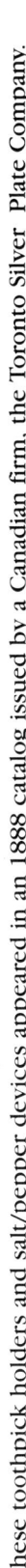

No. 627—SALT.
With Spoon.
Crystal or Blue Glass, $2.75 (*Cluck*)
Canary or Ruby Glass, 3.00 (*Clod*)

No. 703—
TOOTHPICK HOLDER.
$1.00 (*Coat*)

No. 1060.
INDIVIDUAL PEPPER.
$2.50 (*Cloud*)

No. 701—TOOTHPICK HOLDER.
Gold Lined, $3.25 (*Cloy*)

No. 1059.
INDIVIDUAL PEPPER.
80c. (*Close*)

No. 702—
TOOTHPICK HOLDER.
Gold Lined, $2.25 (*Clutch*)

No. 1055—INDIVIDUAL PEPPER.
$1.50 (*Cleft*)

No. 630—SALT
With Spoon.
Crystal Cut Glass.
$2.50 (*Clime*)

No. 704—TOOTHPICK HOLDER.
$1.00 (*Coat*)

No. 700—TOOTHPICK HOLDER.
Gold Lined, $2.25 (*Clove*)

These toothpick holders and salt/pepper devices appeared in an 1888 catalog issued by a Canadian firm, the Toronto Silver Plate Company.

TOOTHPICK HOLDERS

No. 70. Polished, Gold Lined $1.25	No. 82. Butler Finish, Gold Lined $1.25
No. 71. Satin with Polished Top 1.50	No. 85. Satin, Bright Cut, Gold Lined 1.40

MUSTARD POTS

No. 1706. Plain Burnished, Ruby Glass Lining $2.50	No. 1707. Plain Burnished, Ruby Glass Lining $2.50

These toothpick holders and mustard pots appeared in a 1910 catalog (entitled "Hollowware") which was issued by the Rockford Silver Plate Company of Rockford, Illinois.

512. DOULTON. Marked "Shelley" (this mark used from 1925 to present by Royal Doulton). Souvenir "City of Lincoln".

513. GOSS. Marked. Scroll says "Buxton".

514. GOSS. Marked and shows "Rd #521971", a 1908 design registry number.

515. GOSS. Marked. Scroll says "Langport".

516. GOSS TYPE. No mark. Scroll says "London, 1908."

517. GOSS. Marked. Scroll says "Llandudno".

518. GOSS TYPE. Marked with green crown and Czechoslovakia.

519. GOSS TYPE. Marked "Loche & Co." Located at Worcester, England.

520. GOSS. Marked. Different crest on each face.

521. GOSS TYPE. Marked "Botolph, J.W. & Co."

522. ROYAL DOULTON. Mark is lion over crown (begun in 1929).

523. GOSS TYPE.

524. CHINA. Marked "G D A FRANCE." Made by Gerard Dutraissex & Abbot, Limoges, France. Mark used since 1937. Ref: K-NDM #175n.

525. CHINA. Marked "Weimar" across a striped shield and "Germany" below that. Mark was used 1918-1945 by C. & E. Carstens Porcelain Factory Blankenhain, located at Blankenhain, Thuringia, Germany.

526. CHINA. Marked with one of the "Zsolnay Pecs" marks which includes five church towers. Made by Zsolnay at Pecs, Hungary.

527. CHINA. Marked "Favrele, Bavaria." Maker and date unknown. Favrele could be an artist, maker, town or region.

528. CHINA. Marked with a crown, "BEAUTY ROSE" and "PRUSSIA". Maker and date unknown.

529. PORCELAIN. Marked "C.S.PRUSSIA", blue mark, with four petal flower.

530. CHINA. Marked with a wreath similar to Noritake mark with "I", a diamond type symbol and "E" across the inside. "Hand Painted" and "Japan". Made after 1918.

531. CHINA. Marked with a symbol in a wreath similar to the Noritake "N" symbol. Marked "HOHUTOCHA" and "Made in Occupied Japan". Circa 1945-1952.

532. CHINA. Marked "BAVARIA" with logo that looks like a hammer. Probable maker is Plankenhammer Porcelain Factory, Plankenhammer, Bavaria, Germany between 1920 and 1978. Ref: K-NDM #135M is similar.

533. CHINA. Marked with green "J.P." over a line and "L" underneath and "FRANCE". The maker is La Ceramique (Jean Pouyat) Limoges, France. Ref: K-NDM #183c.

534. CHINA. Gaudy Welsh. Marked "MADE IN ENGLAND" with a banner and shield design logo.

535. CHINA. Portrait of Queen Louise. Maker and date unknown.

536. MAJOLICA. Pottery marked only with "1660."

537. PORCELAIN. Marked "VICTORIA, CARLSBAD" in an oval shaped logo with a bird shaped figure in the center. Made by Victoria Porcelain Factory, Altrohlau, Bohemia, (Stara Role Czechoslovakia). Mark used 1891-1918. Ref: K-NDM #59M.

538. CHINA. Marked "WHEELOCK CHINA, AUSTRIA", in a circle logo that has a crown on the top and a "W" in the center.

539. PORCELAIN. Marked with a crossed lines symbol that has "R" and "C" to the left and right respectively and a crown above. This mark was used by the Philip Rosenthal & Co. and Rosenthal Porcelain AG, Kronach, Bavaria, Germany from 1901 to 1956. Below the mark is printed "CRYSANTHESE, BAVARIA". Rosenthal Porcelain A.G. is the modern corporate name. Ref: K-NDM #83E.

540. CHINA. Maker and date unknown.

541. CHINA. Marked "PROV, SAXE, E.S. GERMANY", the mark of Erdmann Schlegelmilch, a company located in Suhl, Thuringia, Germany.

542. CHINA. Mark not fully legible. Made in Austria.

543. CHINA. Maker and date unknown.

544. CHINA. Marked "MADE IN CZECHOSLOVAKIA."

545. CHINA. Marked "LORD & TAYLOR", a department store chain currently owned by the May Co. Maker and date unknown.

546. CHINA. Souvenir of "WAPAKONETA, OHIO." Maker and date unknown.

547. CHINA. Marked "GERMANY" with a green stamp in script. Maker and date unknown.

548. CHINA. Marked "COALPORT PORCELAIN WORKS, COALPORT, ENGLAND." Rd # (Design Registry Number) seems to read 118792, issued in 1889. Just under 2" tall, very thin and translucent. Ref: K-NDM #88N.

549. CHINA. No mark. Maker and date unknown.

550. CHINA. Marked "LEFTON CHINA, HAND PAINTED" and "REG.U.S.PAT.OFF." with a crown. Mark used 1949-1955. Lefton is a U.S. importer. Ref: L-USM.

551. CHINA. Marked "BAVARIA" and "42" incised in base. Maker and date unknown.

552. PORCELAIN. Three handles. Marked with black mark "Beleek" stamp. Lustre finish.

553. CHINA. Marked "MADE IN GERMANY" in a rectangular box. Three handled, 2" high. Maker and date unknown.

554. CHINA. Marked with a script "L" and some other undetermined letters along with "DANMARK". Maker and date unknown.

555. CHINA. Thin, fine quality. Maker and date unknown.

556. BISQUE. Decorated. Maker and date unknown. Same shape as H-R/U #1438.

557. PORCELAIN. Marked with red printed mark of Royal Crown, "DERBY, ENGLAND", "1502" and cypher for year. Circa 1912. Made by Royal Crown Derby Porcelain, Ltd. of Derby, England. Ref: G-BPPM page 203 #1270.

558. PORCELAIN. Marked "R.S. Germany." Maker and date unknown. Same as #459.

559. CHINA. Marked "EPIAG RICH, CHESCHO-SLOVCIDA". 2 1/2" high. Brass holder.

560. CHINA. Marked faintly with "65." Fine quality porcelain. Identified only as "probably French" at the 1990 NTHCS convention. Maker and date unknown.

561. CHINA. Marked "Hand Painted - Japan." Made after 1921. Maker unknown.

562. CHINA. Portrait is embossed. Maker and date unknown.

563. CHINA. Appears to be hand painted. Has a false bottom and lustre interior. Maker and date unknown.

564. CHINA. R.S. Prussia, unmarked. Ref: G-RSI plate 546.

565. CHINA. Cobalt blue and cream with a gold design. Keyhole shape cutout on side. Maker and date unknown.

566. PORCELAIN. Probably R.S. Prussia per Wm. Heacock. Similar to a red mark R.S. Prussia holder shown in T-RSP page 98. Ref: H-1000 #428.

567. CHINA. Marked "24 karat" in crested gold and platinum. It is gold inside, has five panels with flowers in gold and one panel showing two people. Design appears to be etched. Maker and date unknown.

568. PORCELAIN. This shoe came from a table set marked "NIPPON". Maker and date unknown.

569. CHINA. Maker and date unknown.

570. MORIAGE. Maker and date unknown.

571. PORCELAIN. Tapestry. Not marked. Probably German or Austrian, circa 1920. Ref: H-1000 #464.

572. MORIAGE. Maker and date unknown.

573. PORCELAIN. Fairyland Lustre. Fruits pattern. Marked "WEDGWOOD, ETRURIA, ENGLAND." Inside is Mother of Pearl color with gold highlights and fruits in the base. Circa 1905. Ref: H-1000 #462 and H-R/U #1429.

574. PORCELAIN. Marked "WEMBLEY-1924." It appears to be Wedgwood Jasperware in black.

575. CHINA. Unmarked. Unconfirmed Royal Worcester attribution. Royal Worcester Spode, Ltd. of England is a conglomerate of several old companies.

576. PORCELAIN. Fairyland Lustre. Dragons in design. A dragon is on the inside bottom. See #573 above. Ref: H-1000 #462 and H-R/U #1429.

577. PORCELAIN. Marked "Wedgwood." Blue background, white relief. Greek scene.

578. PORCELAIN. Marked "WEDGWOOD, MADE IN ENGLAND" with a carat mark and an "X". Appears to be Jasperware. Probably a match holder.

579. PORCELAIN. Marked "WEDGWOOD, ENGLAND". Jasperware.

580. CHINA. Marked "UNSTAL ENGLAND, ADAMS, ESTBS 1657". ("UNSTAL" is probably an incomplete "TUNSTALL".) Wm. Adams & Sons is presently part of the Wedgwood group.

581. PORCELAIN. Marked "DOULTON, LAMBETH, ENGLAND".

582. CHINA. Marked "ADAMS, ESTBD 1657, 349, TUNSTALL, ENGLAND." Jasperware. Adams is presently part of the Wedgwood group.

583. CHINA. Marked "ADAMS" and made in Tunstall, England. Jasperware.

584. CHINA. Marked "ADAMS, TUNSTALL, ENGLAND." Jasperware.

585. POTTERY. Marked "PAINCESS, IVORA, GOUDA." Colors on this Art Nouveau style are blue, white, and orange, and the interior is black. Circa 1895-1910. Gouda is a province in The Netherlands noted for colorful pottery.

586. PORCELAIN. Marked "DUDSON-HANLEY" on the inside. Possibly Dudson, Wilcox & Till, Ltd. of Hanley, Staffordshire, England from 1902 to 1926.

587. PORCELAIN. Marked "MADE IN IRELAND." Made by Wade, Ireland, Ltd., circa 1960's-1970's. Advertised as a violet bowl. Ref: WP-W.

588. POTTERY. Gouda. Marked "476, WEGA, X" and ten slash marks across the center of the bottom. Appears to be Art Nouveau pottery in a matte finish typical of 1895-1910.

589. CHINA. Boating scene marked "MEAUN; C.P./& CO." in an eight-sided logo, and "FRANCE". Made by Charles Pillivuyt at Mehun-Sur-Yevre, France. Ref: K-NDM #1510.

590. CHINA. Marked "THE FOLEY CHINA, ENGLAND, 27, 1776." This mark was used by Wileman & Co. of Fenton and London, England, 1892-1925.

591. CHINA. "BRENNEN & FITZGERALD." This may be the distributor. The text with the Indian is "PENOBSCOT INN". An example of souvenir ware.

592. CHINA. Marked "MADE IN GERMANY" in a circular logo. The shield says "SOME OF THE FISHING SCHRS, FREEPORT, N.J."

593. CHINA. Marked "DELFT Germany" with crossed pipes. Delft is a term applied to a type of 18th, 19th and 20th century pottery. References show this term used by many American and Dutch firms. Delft is still made. Also see #618.

594. CHINA. Delft type. See #593 above.

595. CHINA. Not marked.

596. CHINA. Marked "GERMANY" inside a sawtoothed oval.

597. CHINA. Marked "ROYAL SAXE" over a crown and "GERMANY." The Indian is Sitting Bull.

598. CHINA. Cobalt souvenir ware. Marked "MADE IN GERMANY" around the top of an oval. Marked "GOIE MARA PNAWDLE" in a bar across the oval. Presumed to be the name of the Indian shown.

599. CHINA. Marked "ROYAL SAXE" over a crown and "GERMANY." The Indian is High Hawk.

600. CHINA. Marked "MADE IN GERMANY FOR COPPER CITY COMMERCIAL MARKET, ANACONDA, MONT." The legend under the Indian says "FLAT HEADED INDIAN CHIEF, ANACONDA, MONT."

601. CHINA. Note the shape has eight small feet. No marks. Believed to be recent (1980's).

602. CHINA. Paper label says "A.S. COOPER & SONS, LTD. HAMILTON, BERMUDA." Probably an importer. Marked "B & G", Kjobenhavn, a trademark of Bing & Grohndahl, Denmark.

603. CHINA. Marked "DUPPEL MUHLE." Boat with eggshell and Dutch windmill scene. Mark is probably a souvenir legend.

604. CHINA. Marked "W.A. PICKARD, HAND PAINTED CHINA" in a circular logo. Pickard is located in Chicago, Illinois. This logo was used 1895-1898. Ref: K-NDM #49D.

605. PORCELAIN. Marked "PORCELAINE de PARIS, FRANCE" with a crossed arrows logo. Made by R. Bloch Porcelain of Paris, France. Mark used since 1954. Ref: K-NDM #17H.

606. CHINA. Marked "SPODE'S CAMILLA, COPELAND, ENGLAND."

607. CHINA. Marked with a six point star and "LIMOGES, FRANCE". Maker not identified.

608. CHINA. Unmarked. Identified by Orva Heisenbuttal as "early Haviland".

609. CHINA. Tri-cornered shape. Marked with Crown and World mark used by Minton.

610. CHINA. Marked "JANROTH, GERMANY." Cobalt souvenir of State Monument at Gettysburg, Pa.

611. PORCELAIN. Mark of Worcester Royal Porcelain Co. Ltd., Worcester, England. Age uncertain. Ref: K-NDM page 255.

612. CHINA. Possibly Mettlach. No information on mark was provided.

613. CHINA. Marked "HAND PAINTED CHINA, W. PICKARD" in a circular logo. Circa 1895-1898. Ref: K-NDM #149D.

614. CHINA. Marked "HAVILAND."

615. PORCELAIN. Marked with logo of Worcester Royal Porcelain Co. Ltd. Ref: K-NDM page 255.

616. CHINA. Marked "COPELAND, SPODE'S, ITALIAN, ENGLAND." The words are printed in an oval.

617. PORCELAIN. Marked with logo of W.T. Copeland & Sons, Ltd., Stoke, Staffordshire, England. Mark used 1851-1885. Unusual combination of cream colored porcelain with flow blue coloring. Ref: K-NDM #133D.

618. PORCELAIN. Marked Delft-Germany. The symbol is a combination of the Delft Jug with superimposed crossed pipes. Also see 593.

619. CHINA. Marked "CROWN DUCAL WARE ENGLAND" with a crown over the words. Ref: K-NDM #87F.

620. HAT. Van Briggle, marked with double back-to-back "A" trademark in a square. Probably circa 1940.

621. POTTERY. Niloak Pottery Co. of Benton, Arkansas.

622. POTTERY. Hand made, salt glazed by Williamsburg Pottery Factory in Rightfoot, Va. Company is known for "Colonial Williamsburg Foundation" and "Williamsburg Restoration Foundation" items. Probably circa 1980's.

623. POTTERY. Niloak. Swirled pottery like this is difficult to produce.

624. ART NOUVEAU POTTERY. Watcombe Pottery, South Devon, England.

625. POTTERY. Possibly "Pearl" by Weller Pottery, Zanesville, Ohio, circa 1910. There are shape and design differences with items shown in H-WEL, page 177, that make this a questionable attribution.

626. POTTERY. Green stump signed "OHR." Made by George Ohr, known as "the mad potter of Biloxi (Mississippi)." Circa 1884-1915.

627. POTTERY. Possibly Van Briggle. No mark indicated.

628. CHINA. Marked "LEFTON CHINA." Imported since 1940's, probably from Japan.

629. CHINA. Crested or Goss type holder. Marked with a crown over a wave-like line, "B.R.C." and "BERMUDA LOVING CUP." Rim is silver. The mark has not been identified. Same as #687.

630. CHINA. Marked "ROSENTHAL." Has platinum trim. Rosenthal is still in business.

631. CHINA. Possibly Foley China, England. No mark described.

632. METAL. Enameled copper. Possibly Battersea, a term for enamel on metal objects of the 18th century. This seems more like 19th or 20th century. Research continues.

633. CHINA. Marked with crown above circle mark of Royal Worcester and "3203." Made by Worcester of Worcester, England.

634. CHINA. Marked "W & R, STOKE ON TRENT, CARLTON CHINA" and a crown on a circle logo, "184" and "N". The maker is Wiltshaw & Robinson Ltd., Carlton Works, Stoke, England, one of the Staffordshire potteries.

635. CHINA. Marked "DRESDEN" with logo that appears to be feathers turned outward, joined near base with a crossbar. Features a different floral pattern on each of the four sides.

636. MAJOLICA. Sanitary or lay down holder. Ear of corn. Numbered.

637. MAJOLICA. Sanitary or lay down holder. Cucumber. Numbered.

638. MAJOLICA. Sanitary or lay down holder. Fish. Numbered.

639. CHINA. Hyde pattern. Made by Woods, Burslem, England. Marked "ENOCH 1784; RALPH 1750" in addition to maker's name. Logo used since 1931. Ref: K-NDM #127L.

640. CHINA. Sanitary type with transfer print. Looks like "TK" inscribed in one end of base.

641. CHINA. Bone china. Maker and date unknown.

642. CHINA. Marked "GERMANY, 10101" over "53" with another mark only partly visible.

643. CHINA. Rose spray inside as well as outside. Maker and date unknown.

644. CHINA. Marked "RIDGWAYS, ENGLAND." Dutch scene. Sailboats on one side, windmills on the other. Scene is signed "HOHFLEUR FISHING BOATS." Ref: K-NDM #138L except the words "Royal Semi Porcelain" do not appear as part of the mark.

645. CHINA. Marked "K-L" in a simple circle and "Bavaria." Same shape as #643.

646. CHINA. Marked "H & G BAVARIA" over a crown logo.

647. CHINA. Figural. No mark. Maker and date unknown.

648. CHINA. Figural. No mark. Maker and date unknown.

649. CHINA. Figural. Marked "C" in a circle, "L & M INC." 4" tall. Container is 1 3/4" deep.

650. BISQUE. Figural. 2 1/2" tall. No mark. Maker and date unknown.

651. CHINA. Figural. Maker and date unknown.

652. CHINA. Figural. Maker and date unknown.

653. BISQUE. Figural. Maker and date unknown.

654. BISQUE. Figural. Marked "FRANCE". Maker and date unknown.

655. CHINA. Figural. Marked "GERMANY" in script. Says "BOSTON BAKED BEANS."

656. BISQUE. Figural. Maker and date unknown.

657. CHINA. Figural. Marked "GERMANY." Maker and date unknown.

658. CHINA. Figural. Maker and date unknown.

659. CHINA. Figural. Maker and date unknown.

660. CHINA. Figural. Maker and date unknown.

661. CHINA. Figural. Maker and date unknown.

662. CHINA. Figural. Maker and date unknown.

663. BISQUE. Figural. 4 1/2" tall. Maker and date unknown.

664. BISQUE. Figural. Maker and date unknown.

665. BISQUE. Figural. Rooster on wooden legs. Has crown mark of Schafer & Vater and "9160."

666. BISQUE. Figural. 5 1/4" tall. Maker and date unknown.

667. BISQUE. Figural. Maker and date unknown.

668. BISQUE. Figural. Marked "OCCUPIED JAPAN." 4 1/2" tall.

669. BISQUE. Figural. 4" tall. Maker and date unknown.

670. BISQUE. Figural. Maker and date unknown.

671. BISQUE. Figural. Maker and date unknown.

672. BISQUE. Figural. Maker and date unknown.

673. BISQUE. Figural. Maker and date unknown.

674. BISQUE. Figural. The holder is behind the sailor and girl. Possibly Schafer & Vater.

675. BISQUE. Figural. Container 1 1/2"tall, elf 3 1/2" tall. Maker and date unknown.

676. BISQUE. Figural. Maker and date unknown.

677. BISQUE. Figural. Maker and date unknown.

678. BISQUE. Figural. Maker and date unknown.

679. BISQUE. Figural. Marked with an anchor and "1801 EBS". Maker and date uncertain. Possibly from Holland.

680. BISQUE. Figural. Marked "GERMANY" with a number. Maker and date unknown.

681. BISQUE. Figural. Egg is 2 1/2" tall, rabbit is 3" tall. Maker and date unknown.

682. MAJOLICA. Three faced gargoyle. Colors of blue, green and brown. Maker and date unknown.

683. CHINA. Umbrella. Maker and date unknown.

684. CHINA. Souvenir. Marked "MADE IN AUSTRIA" and "MADE FOR M.R. SINKS." Shows old state capitol at Jefferson City, Mo.

685. CHINA. Marked "ELECTROLYTIC E.A.M. CO., TRENTON, NEW JERSEY." Decorated in silver. Detail of etching in silver leaves and flowers is lost in the photo.

686. CHINA. Maker and date unknown.

687. CHINA. Souvenir. Stamped "BERMUDA LOVING CUP" on bottom. Marked "B.R.C." under a crown with a wave-like line between. Silver rim. Same as #629.

688. CHINA. Bulldog. Possibly Staffordshire. Date unknown.

689. CHINA. Cobalt souvenir. Marked with circle that has "J.H.R. & Co." in the center, "ROYAL ROTHENBURG" and a "G" in a ring around that, a crown on top of the circle and "GERMANY" below the circle. Maker and date not identified.

690. CHINA. Souvenir. Marked with "VICTORIA, CARLSBAD" in an oval ring around a bird like figure. Made by Victoria Porcelain Factory of Atrohlau, Bohemia (Stara Role, Czechoslovakia) between 1891 and 1918. Ref: K-NDM #59M.

691. CHINA. "22" incised on bottom. Maker and date unknown.

692. BISQUE. Unglazed. Maker and date unknown.

693. CHINA. Note the mouse. Screen painted. The shape suggests other than a toothpick or match holder. Maker and date unknown.

694. CHINA. Silver rim (possibly sterling). Maker and date unknown.

695. CHINA. Charles & Diana miniature loving cup. Made by Wade in England, circa 1981. Commemorative of the Royal Wedding. Ref: WP-W #677.

696. CHINA. Royal family: Queen Elizabeth, Prince Charles and Princess Diana, Prince William and Prince Harry. Marked with a crown and "CORONET POTTERY" which is located in Staffordshire, England.

697. CHINA. Marked with a ship logo. The sails say "FURNIVALS LIMITED." Underneath is "ENGLAND." Furnivals is located at Corbridge, Staffordshire, England, however the word "DENMARK" appears above the sail. Ref: K-NDM #134H.

698. SILVERPLATE. Figural. Marked "JAMES W. TUFTS, BOSTON, WARRANTED, TRIPLE PLATE, 2645." Circa 1890. Ref: H-R/ U p. 95.

699. SILVERPLATE. Figural. Marked "JAMES W. TUFTS, BOSTON, WARRANTED, QUADRUPLE PLATE, 3404." Circa 1890.

700. SILVERPLATE. Figural. Marked "JAMES W. TUFTS, BOSTON, WARRANTED, QUADRUPLE PLATE, 3403." Circa 1890. Ref: H-R/U page 94.

701. SILVERPLATE. Figural. Marked "MERIDEN B COMPANY, QUADRUPLE PLATE, 22." Circa 1886. Ref: R-ASP page 357.

702. SILVERPLATE. Figural. Marked "39 GILL." Circa 1885. Curious cat is peeking into holder.

703. SILVERPLATE. Figural. Marked "SOUTHINGTON C COMPANY, QUADRUPLE PLATE, 2." Circa 1887.

704. SILVERPLATE. Figural. Marked "MERIDEN SILVER." Circa 1890. Squirrel eating an acorn.

705. SILVERPLATE. Figural. Marked "JAMES W. TUFTS, BOSTON, WARRANTED, QUADRUPLE PLATE, 3411." Circa 1890's. Hissing cat.

706. SILVERPLATE. Figural. Marked "WILCOX SILVER PLATE CO., MERIDEN, CONN., 2863." Circa 1900.

707. SILVERPLATE. Figural. Marked "BABCOCK & CO., QUADRUPLE PLATE." Circa 1890's. Ref: HJ-S #4306 shows this as an open salt.

708. SILVERPLATE. Figural. Marked "MIDDLETOWN SILVER CO." Circa 1890. The figure is a fox.

709. SILVERPLATE. Figural. Marked "WILCOX SILVER PLATE CO." Circa 1900. Has a violin on one side and a top hat on the other. See #860 for a similar holder.

710. SILVERPLATE. Figural. Marked "ST. LOUIS SILVER CO." in a circle. Circa 1900.

711. SILVERPLATE. Figural. Marked "ROCKFORD SILVER PLATE CO. 41." Circa 1885.

712. SILVERPLATE. Figural. Marked "W B" in a shield and "2634." Circa 1900's. Possibly a mustard. Probably the Weidlich Bros. Mfg. Co.

713. SILVERPLATE. Figural. Marked "MADE IN JAPAN". Indian with barrel on back.

714. SILVERPLATE. Figural. Marked "PAIRPOINT, NEW BEDFORD, 3703." Circa 1890's. Figure is oriental. 2 1/4" high.

715. SILVERPLATE. Figural. Marked "O K CO". Circa 1915. A "K" over an "O" is part of the Kronheimer Oldenbusch & Co. (New York) mark.

716. SILVERPLATE. Figural. Maker unknown. Possibly circa 1890's. Cherub on a pedestal.

717. SILVERPLATE. Figural. Marked "MIDDLETOWN PLATE CO., QUADRUPLE PLATE, 32, HARD WHITE METAL." Circa 1890. Gilt on the inside. Soldier standing guard. Same as #847.

718. SILVERPLATE. Figural. Marked "67 B I/O OX" with a diamond shape in an arch. Maker unknown. Circa 1890.

719. SILVERPLATE. Figural. Barbour Silver Co., circa 1890. Bird on a branch. Ref: H-1000 #794.

720. SILVERPLATE. Figural. Marked "INDUSTRIA ARGENTINA." Maker and date unknown. Three llamas surround the holder.

721. SILVERPLATE. Figural. Maker unknown. Humpty Dumpty.

722. SILVERPLATE. Figural. Marked "WILCOX SILVER PLATE CO." Circa 1890.

723. SILVERPLATE. Figural. Maker unknown. Circa 1890. Figure is a monkey.

724. SILVERPLATE. Figural. Maker unknown. Circa 1885. Man leaning on pine cone with holes for picks.

725. SILVERPLATE. Figural. Marked "JAMES W. TUFTS-2694." Circa 1890. The bird is a parrot. Ref: H-R/U page 95.

726. SILVERPLATE. Figural. Marked "MERIDEN COMPANY" around a balance scale mark and "QUADRUPLE PLATE." Circa 1886.

727. SILVERPLATE. Figural. Marked "AURORA SILVER PLATE CO." Circa 1890.

728. SILVERPLATE. Figural. Marked "MANUFACTURED AND PLATED, SIMPSON, H. M. CO., USA 0807." Circa 1890. It reads "Kind Wishes."

729. SILVERPLATE. Figural. Marked "DERBY SILVER, QUADRUPLE PLATE" in a ring around anchor mark and "1730." Circa 1885. Also seen without the child. See 924.

730. SILVERPLATE. Figural. Marked "POOLE SILVER CO." in a ring with "QUADRUPLE PLATE, TAUNTON, MASS." around that ring. Circa 1890.

731. SILVERPLATE. Figural. Marked "MERIDEN B COMPANY" in a ring around a balance scale inside a shield. Circa 1890. This monkey-like figure holds a lantern that swings.

732. SILVERPLATE. Figural. Marked "ROCKFORD SILVER P CO. QUADRUPLE PLATE." Circa 1890.

733. SILVERPLATE. Figural. Marked "POOLE SILVER CO." Circa 1890.

734. SILVERPLATE. Figural. Marked "W T M F." Made by Wittenbergische Metallware Fabriki, Geislingen, Germany. Gnome lighting a pipe.

735. SILVERPLATE. Figural. Marked "4 x 14". Maker unknown. Egg is etched "MATE". Probably a salt dip or an egg cup. Circa 1890.

736. SILVERPLATE. Figural. Marked "WARRANTED QUADRUPLE PLATE, 212." Crouching dog with "Take Your Pick" incised on the holder. Circa 1890.

737. SILVERPLATE. Figural. Marked "ACME SILVER CO." Possibly Canadian between 1885 and 1893.

738. SILVERPLATE. Figural. Marked "JAMES W. TUFTS, QUADRUPLE PLATE, BOSTON, WARRANTED, 3460." Circa 1890's.

739. SILVERPLATE. Marked "PAIRPOINT MFG. CO. NEW BEDFORD, MASS. QUADRUPLE PLATE 3731." It reads "Handy Picks of Wood." Circa 1894. Ref: PMCC

740. SILVERPLATE. Figural. Marked "37." Maker unknown. Probably circa 1890's.

741. SILVERPLATE. Figural. Maker unknown. Pictured as a match holder in *Sterling Silver, Silver, Silverplate and Souvenir Spoons with Prices*, July, 1977 by L-W Inc., Gas City, Indiana. Circa 1880's. Cupid inscribed "Peek-A-Boo".

742. SILVERPLATE. Figural. Marked "MIDDLETOWN PLATE CO. QUADRUPLE PLATE, 37, HARD WHITE METAL, B.C." Circa 1890. Inscribed "Good Morning". Rabbit is nibbling wheat.

743. SILVERPLATE. Figural. Marked "MERIDEN SILVER." Circa 1890. Note ornate handles.

744. SILVERPLATE. Figural. Marked "C" on bottom of log foot. Circa 1900.

745. SILVERPLATE. Marked Pairpoint. Circa 1894. With an axe laid across it, it would match a part of the 4905 smoke set in PMCC.

746. SILVERPLATE. Marked Pairpoint. Circa 1894. This is part of the #4907 smoke set illustrated in PMCC.

747. SILVERPLATE. Figural. Marked "WILLIAM A. ROGERS, 402." Circa 1890.

748. BRASS. Maker unknown. May have been plated at one time. Circa 1885.

749. SILVERPLATE. Marked "DERBY SILVER CO., QUADRUPLE PLATE, 2314."

750. SILVERPLATE. Marked Pairpoint. Circa 1890.

751. SILVERPLATE. Marked "AURORA S.P. CO." Circa 1890.

752. SILVERPLATE. Marked inside "VICTOR SILVER." Bottom marked "PAT'D MAY 22, 1903, DERBY SILVER CO., QUADRUPLE PLATE, 1779." Applied flower.

753. SILVERPLATE. Marked "ROGERS M I T, QUADRUPLE PLATE, 34, USA." Circa 1900's.

754. SILVERPLATE. Marked "WILCOX SILVER PLATE CO., MERIDEN, CONN., QUADRUPLE PLATE, GILT, 6103" with crossed hammers. Circa 1890's.

755. SILVERPLATE. Marked "WILCOX SILVER PLATE CO., MERIDEN, CONN., QUADRUPLE PLATE, GILT, 6113" with crossed hammers. Shown in an 1880's catalog reprint by Gilded Age Press as a "pen wiper".

756. SILVERPLATE. Marked "E.G. WEBSTER & SON, N.Y., 33" around the arm and hammer mark. Circa 1890's.

757. SILVERPLATE. Maker unknown. Probably circa 1890.

758. SILVERPLATE. Three footed sanitary. Maker unknown. Probably circa 1900.

759. SILVERPLATE. The markings are hallmark-like with "H.H." in the center of the mark. A mark like an inverted "V" in a pentagon precedes and "90" follows. Maker unknown. Circa 1900.

760. SILVERPLATE. Figural. Marked "DERBY" 7 1/2" tall, basket is 2 1/2" tall. Circa 1890.

761. SILVERPLATE. Figural. Marked "JAMES W. TUFTS, BOSTON, WARRANTED TRIP PLATE, 848." Circa 1890's. Ref: H-R/U p. 95.

762. STERLING SILVER. Figural. Artist signed.

763. STERLING SILVER. Marked "BLACK, STAR AND FROST", a N.Y. jewelry company. It is stamped "DINNER OF THE FIRST PANEL, SHERIFF'S JURY, JAN. 14, 1897." Ref: RH-CE.

764. PEWTER. The mark is that of Hanle & Debler, Inc. founded in 1933 and purchased by Kirk Corp. in 1971. Noted for colonial reproductions of distinctive American pewter. Possibly a cigarette holder based on shape and age.

765. STERLING SILVER. English hallmarks. Handles are gargoyles.

766. STERLING SILVER. May be a cigarette holder.

767. SILVERPLATE. This has the Pairpoint mark and "3713." Same as #923.

768. STERLING SILVER. Marked "STERLING". May be a cigarette holder of 1930's to 1970's vintage.

769. SILVERPLATE. Marked "B SILVER PLATE." Has a glass insert and 3 ball feet. Circa 1910. This was advertised as a toothpick holder, but without the feet.

770. STERLING SILVER. Described as "sterling, reinforced with cement with English markings". The shape suggests a 1930's-1970's cigarette holder with weighted base to prevent tipping.

771. SILVERPLATE. Marked "PAIRPOINT, 4186, SHEFFIELD, MADE IN USA" and the Pairpoint mark. The 1894 cataloged Pairpoint holders are numbered in the 3700 series and mustard pots are in the 4100 series (4150's in 1894). That plus the fact that most mustard pots shown are glass lined, leads to the conclusion that this item was probably originally made as a mustard.

772. STERLING SILVER. Marked with hallmark and "STERLING B6254." In this shape, with a glass liner, it may be a mustard. Probably 1910 or later.

773. SILVERPLATE. Marked "SIMPSON, HALL & MILLER, 109, QUADRUPLE PLATE". Repousse design. Circa 1890.

774. STERLING SILVER. Marked "REED & BARTON X 57". Circa 1900.

775. STERLING SILVER. Marked "MERMOD & JACCARD JEWELRY CO., STERLING, 426." Circa 1890's.

776. SILVERPLATE. Marked "SHEFFIELD" with an unidentified hallmark. Circa 1910.

777. SILVERPLATE. Figural. Marked "AURORA CO., S.P. MFG." around the number "327." Circa 1890.

778. SILVERPLATE. Figural. Gargoyle with basket. Marked "MERIDEN B COMPANY" and "3" with balance scale mark. Circa 1885.

779. SILVERPLATE. Marked "AURORA SPMF CO., QUADRUPLE PLATE, WARRANTED, 344." Circa 1890.

780. SILVERPLATE. Figural. Marked "MFD & PLATED BY REED & BARTON, 355." Circa 1885.

781. SILVERPLATE. Marked "JAMES W. TUFTS, 3414." Circa 1890's.

782. SILVERPLATE. Embossed. Marked "HOMAN MANUFACTURING CO., QUADRUPLE PLATE, MADE IN USA, 3056" and "SPECIAL H METAL." Circa 1904-1915.

783. SILVERPLATE. Figural. "ROGERS & BROS" mark is probably "C. ROGERS & BROS." Ref: S-NAP shows "MERIDEN SILVER PLATE CO". According to R-EASM, C. Rogers & Bros. used "SO. MERIDEN SILVER CO. QUADRUPLE" on less expensive items around 1899.

784. SILVERPLATE. Marked "HOMAN MFG. CO." Circa 1896. Same as #890.

785. SILVERPLATE. Figural. Marked "MANHATTAN SILVERPLATE CO., QUADRUPLE PLATE" in their star and crescent mark. Circa 1885.

786. SILVERPLATE. Figural. Marked "D.A.R. CO." (the "R" is large) and "76." Circa 1885.

787. SILVERPLATE. Figural. Marked "JAMES W. TUFTS." Circa 1890. The staff or whatever he was originally holding is missing. It may have been a pipe cleaner. Ref: H-R/U page 94, item #3401.

788. SILVERPLATE. Marked "AURORA SILVER PLATE CO." Open work around base and middle. Circa 1890.

789. SILVERPLATE. Marked "JAPAN." Maker and date unknown.

790. SILVERPLATE. Marked "MERIDEN B COMPANY" with their balance scale mark and "QUADRUPLE PLATE" and "40." 2 1/4" high. Circa 1900.

791. SILVERPLATE. No information available.

792. SILVERPLATE. Figural. Has bellows and tongs attached. The inscription is "OLD MEMORIES." Maker unknown. Circa 1890.

793. SILVERPLATE. Figural. Marked "JAMES W. TUFTS 3414." Circa 1890's.

794. SILVERPLATE. Figural. Marked "M S P CO., 083." This is a type of squirrel. Circa 1890.

795. SILVERPLATE. Figural. Marked "MERIDEN SILVER PLATE CO." Circa 1892.

796. SILVERPLATE. Figural. Marked "ROGERS SMITH & CO. MERIDEN, CONN., QUADRUPLE PLATE" over a shield mark. Appears to be a Kate Greenaway-type figure. Circa 1885.

797. SILVERPLATE. Figural. No mark. Interior of shell is gilt. Movable parts were rare in 1890. Circa 1890.

798. SILVERPLATE. Figural. No mark. Base and bear are pewter. Holder is silverplated. Circa 1890.

799. SILVERPLATE. Figural. Possibly James W. Tufts. A sanitary holder with movable parts. Circa 1890.

800. SILVERPLATE. Figural. Chick and butterfly with basket. Marked "JAMES W. TUFTS, BOSTON, MASS. 2697." Ref: H-R/U page 95.

801. SILVERPLATE. Figural. Conquistador holding torch. No marks. Circa 1885.

802. SILVERPLATE. Figural. Nude Arab holding half an egg shell standing over half an egg shell beside a chick. No marks. Circa 1890.

803. SILVERPLATE. Figural. Apple on tray has holes for toothpicks. No mark. Circa 1885.

804. SILVERPLATE. Figural. Marked "DERBY SILVER CO. QUADRUPLE PLATE, 2300." Circa 1885.

805. SILVERPLATE. Figural. Little wishbone on the tray doesn't show very well. Marked "SIMPSON, HALL, MILLER & CO. QUADRUPLE PLATE, 0804." Circa 1905.

806. SILVERPLATE. Figural. Marked "REED & BARTON 225." Ref: R-ASP ad reprint of 1885 catalog.

807. SILVERPLATE. Figural. Frog in tuxedo is marked "REED & BARTON, 350." Ref: R-ASP ad reprint of 1885 catalog.

808. SILVERPLATE. Figural. Marked "SIMPSON, HALL, MILLER & CO. QUADRUPLE PLATE." Circa 1900.

809. SILVERPLATE. Figural. Marked "WM. ROGERS MFG. CO., ROGERS, HARTFORD, CONN." S-NAP shows a napkin ring with this design attributed to "West Silver Co." which was absorbed by Rogers prior to 1896.

810. SILVERPLATE. Figural. Marked "WILCOX SILVER CO. 2632." Probably a match holder with ashtray. Circa 1900.

811. SILVERPLATE. Figural. Marked "MERIDEN B CO. QUADRUPLE PLATE, 54, USA." Bushy-tailed squirrel is playing a horn. Circa 1890.

812. SILVERPLATE. Figural. This angel by a basket has no marks. Circa 1885.

813. SILVERPLATE. Figural. Man with a basket. No marks. Base appears to be silverplate, but the top is yellowish. Possibly brass. Circa 1900.

814. SILVERPLATE. Figural. Marked "REED & BARTON." About 4" tall. Circa 1885.

815. SILVERPLATE. Figural. Maker unknown. Circa 1885.

816. SILVERPLATE. Marked "MERIDEN SILVER PLATE CO." with lion mark and "QUADRUPLE SILVERPLATE 078." Note alternating panels of floral type designs. Circa 1890's.

817. SILVERPLATE. The pattern, "Josephine's Aunt", has openwork at the top and is embossed below. Marked "WESTCOTT SILVER CO." Circa 1900.

818. SILVERPLATE. Marked "MERMOD, JACCARD & CO. ST. LOUIS, MO. 157." This holder was distributed by Mermod, Jaccard & King Jewelry Co. Pictured in Meriden Brittania catalog of 1867 as a salt dip.

819. SILVERPLATE. Figural. The figures (front and back) look like men leaning against a barrel, drinking. No mark.

820. SILVERPLATE. Marked "DERBY SILVER CO." around an anchor over a crown mark. Circa 1890-1910.

821. SILVERPLATE. This has a "K" with an "O" around it, in the triangular mark of Kronheimer Oldenbusch & Co. Circa 1910-1920.

822. SILVERPLATE. Embossed in a shield is "Souvenir of Louisiana Purchase Exposition, St. Louis, Mo. 1904." (1904 St. Louis World's Fair) Made in Germany.

823. SILVERPLATE. Embossed. Marked "PAIRPOINT MFG. CO. NEW BEDFORD, MASS. 4923" with the "P" in a diamond mark. Items numbered in the low 4900's in PMCC were smoking sets. Circa 1890's.

824. SILVERPLATE. Figural. Marked "M B CO" on left foot and "56 USA" on right. Meriden Brittania Co., circa 1885.

825. SILVERPLATE. Figural. Marked "M.S. BENEDICT MFG. CO. QUADRUPLE PLATE 504." 1 3/4" high. Circa late 1890's.

826. SILVERPLATE. Figural. Marked "MADE AND GUARANTEED BY THE VAN BURGH S.P. CO. ROCHESTER, N.Y. USA." Circa 1890's.

827. SILVERPLATE. Figural. Marked "MIDDLETOWN PLATE, QUADRUPLE PLATE, 31, HARD METAL." The figure is a bird on a branch. Circa 1890's.

828. SILVERPLATE. Marked "ROCKFORD SILVER CO. QUADRUPLE, 61" and balance scale logo. 2 1/4" high, 2" across base. Circa 1890's.

829. SILVERPLATE. Figural. Maker unknown. Figure is an old hen, incised "PICKS." Circa 1890's.

830. SILVERPLATE. Figural. A bear. Maker unknown. Tree trunk is 2" high. Circa 1890's.

831. SILVERPLATE. Figural. Marked "JAMES W. TUFTS, BOSTON, MASS. 2896." Crossed ellipses logo. Circa 1894. Ref: H-R/U page 95.

832. SILVERPLATE. Figural. Marked "AURORA S.P. MFG. CO. 328, WARRANTED TRIPLE PLATE." The winged cherub is holding a mandolin. Circa 1890's.

833. SILVERPLATE. Figural. No mark. 1 2/5" high.

834. SILVERPLATE. Figural. No mark. 3" high. Probably circa 1890's.

835. SILVERPLATE. Figural. No mark. 2 3/5" high. Probably circa 1890's. Pot metal, may have been plated.

836. SILVERPLATE. Figural. Unmarked Kate Greenaway-type. Circa 1885.

837. SILVERPLATE. Figural. Front is marked "Yeoman of the Guard." Possibly English with this inscription. Circa 1890.

838. SILVERPLATE. Figural. Unmarked Cupid with egg. Circa 1880's.

839. PEWTER. Figural. A Charles Dickens-type character. Circa 1890.

840. SILVERPLATE. Figural. Marked "MERIDEN B CO. QUADRUPLE PLATE." Dog is sitting up. Circa 1890's.

841. SILVERPLATE. Figural. Marked "GORHAM & CO." This is the name used 1852-1865. Anchor mark and the number 012. Probably for matches during this period.

842. SILVERPLATE. Figural. Marked "MIDDLETOWN PLATE CO., WHITE HARD METAL." Circa 1890.

843. SILVERPLATE. Figural. Marked "SIMPSON, HALL AND MILLER, QUADRUPLE PLATE 26." Circa 1890.

844. SILVERPLATE. Figural. Marked "MERMOD & JACCARD JEWELRY CO. 335." Circa 1901.

845. STERLING SILVER. Figural. Marked "925" and "INDUSTRIA PERUVIA" on the bottom. Circa 1940-1970. Listed as double open salt in HJ-S #4377. May have been for cigarettes and matches.

846. SILVER. Figural. Figure stands on a "Columbian" coin dated 1934. Possibly made in Columbia of coin silver in the 1930's or 1940's. (Coin silver is 90% silver).

847. SILVERPLATE. Figural. Tory soldier standing guard. Marked "MIDDLETOWN PLATE CO. QUADRUPLE PLATE, 32, HARD WHITE METAL GILT." Circa 1890. Same as #717.

848. SILVERPLATE. Two handled with "MAC" on each handle. Souveniring is "The Missouri Athletic Club, St. Louis, Mo. 1903." There are jacks on top of the handles.

849. SILVERPLATE. Marked "PAIRPOINT MFG. CO., NEW BEDFORD, MASS. 3707." 2 1/2" high. Circa 1894. Ref: PMCC

850. SILVERPLATE. Incised front panel says "U.S. BATTLESHIP MAINE DESTROYED IN HAVANA HARBOR, FEB. 15, 1898." A ship and palm tree are shown. Circa 1899.

851. BRASS. No mark. Souvenired "REX - 1903." The handles say "CARNIVAL" and "NEW ORLEANS." Probably a Mardi Gras souvenir. "Rex" is Latin for "King."

852. SILVERPLATE. Figural. Marked "THE DANISH SILVERSMITH" and the initials "REL" and "JHL." Made in Denmark. Circa 1900's.

853. SILVERPLATE. Figural. The underside is marked "TRADEMARK J.B., SIGNIFIES THE BEST 220." Made by Jennings Brass Mfg. Co. Probably circa 1914.

854. SILVERPLATE. Figural. Marked "ROGERS, SMITH & CO. MERIDEN, QUADRAPLATE." Circa 1885.

855. SILVERPLATE. The legs are three birds with their beaks pointing up. Maker unknown. Circa 1900.

856. SILVERPLATE. The front emblem says "H.M.S. HOMERIC." The underside is "R N C S". English.

857. COPPER. No information available. Note the bail. Probably circa 1900.

858. COPPER & BRASS. Design appears to be Indian. Possibly hand tooled from Mexico or another Central/South American country.

859. SILVERPLATE. Mark of Kronheimer Oldenbusch Co. in a triangular shape. The front panel is an attached emblem saying "ST. PAUL, MINN." Circa 1910-1920.

860. SILVERPLATE. Figural. Marked "WILCOX SILVER CO." with crossed hammers in a circle mark. 2 1/4" high. Same holder pictured in S-NAP marked "Meriden Silverplate Co." Both companies were part of International Silver Co., circa 1900. See #709 for a similar item.

861. BRASS. Lightweight. The leaf at right is painted green. The "PICKS" emblem is celluloid. Probably circa 1920's.

862. SILVERPLATE. Figural. Marked "VICTOR SILVER CO. 056." A trademark of Derby Silver Co., circa 1900.

863. SILVERPLATE. Figural. Incised "BEST WISHES." Circa 1900.

864. SILVERPLATE. A fraternal commemorative item. The handles say "32-HOLYROOD, 40-FOREST CITY, and 12-ORIENTAL", which are probably lodges. The bottom is marked "61ST CONCLAVE, GRAND COMMANDERY OF OHIO, KNIGHTS TEMPLARS, CLEVELAND, 803, THE BRENNER BROS. CO. JEWELERS."

865. SILVERPLATE. Figural. Marked with iron cross, "W.R." and a keystone. Made by William Rogers - "half plate", a medium grade for this company. Circa 1900.

866. SILVERPLATE. Figural. Cooper making a barrel. Owner was told that the marks of a dog's head facing to the right and a "B" in a fleur-de-lis outline have been traced to Nuremberg, Germany.

867. PEWTER. Marked "WALLACE PEWTER." Circa 1900.

868. SILVERPLATE. Marked with logo of Kronheimer Oldenbusch Co., circa 1910.

869. SILVERPLATE. Figural. Creeping child with holder on his back. Maker unknown. Probably circa 1885.

870. SILVERPLATE. Figural. Kate Greenaway type. No marks. Probably circa 1885.

871. METAL. Figural. Pot metal. No mark. Circa 1920.

872. SILVERPLATE. Marked "PAIRPOINT MFG. CO. QUADRUPLE PLATE" with "P" in a diamond mark. 2" high. Circa 1894. Also see #891. Ref: PMCC

873. SILVERPLATE. Marked "WOODMAN-COOK CO." which existed 1893-1914.

874. SILVERPLATE. Marked "JAMES W. TUFTS, BOSTON, PLATE GUARANTEED, 3439." Incised design. Circa 1890's.

875. SILVERPLATE. Marked "FORBES SILVER CO. QUADRUPLE, 1910" with eagle's head mark. The incised front says "WAY DOWN EAST" and the back says "100TH PERFORMANCE". Circa 1900.

876. SILVERPLATE. Maker unknown. Has holes to insert picks. Circa 1900.

877. SILVERPLATE. Figural. May be hard white metal, possibly plated. Marked "W.B. MFG. CO., USA." Possibly Weidlich Bros. Circa 1901.

878. SILVERPLATE. Figural. Marked "THE MIDDLETOWN PLATE CO., USA, 305 L 5" with balance scale mark. A figure of a child is soldered to the holder.

879. SILVERPLATE. Marked with a circle with "WARRENTED" and "PLATE" around it. "QUADRUPLE" appears across the circle, and under it is "LANCASTER, PA." Above the circle is something illegible - possibly "OSBORN" - which would be the Osborn Co. of Lancaster, Pa., known to have have used a similar mark. Circa 1898. Ref: R-ASM and Mumford collection.

880. SILVERPLATE. Marked "WOODMAN-COOK CO. PORTLAND, MAINE, QUADRUPLE PLATE, 960." Circa 1893-1914.

881. SILVERPLATE. Probably Kronheimer Oldenbusch Co., circa 1910-1920. A shield with souveniring on it was applied to a basic shape.

882. SILVERPLATE. Figural. Probably cast. Maker and age unknown.

883. SILVERPLATE. Probably foreign. Similar pieces have perfume bottle inserts.

884. SILVERPLATE. Marked "AURORA S.P. MFG. CO. QUADRUPLE PLATED, WARRANTED, 345 1/2." Two part item, engraving on the sides. Insert is 2 1/2" deep. Circa 1886.

885. SILVERPLATE. Marked "MERIDEN B. CO. QUADRUPLE PLATE, 28, USA." (Made by Meriden Brittania Co.) Embossing is called repousse. Circa 1890's.

886. SILVERPLATE. Marked "DERBY SILVER CO. QUADRUPLE PLATE." Anchor over a crown mark. 2 1/2" high. Circa 1900.

887. SILVERPLATE. Marked "LION SILVER CO. QUADRUPLE PLATE." Circa 1890.

888. SILVERPLATE. Marked "DERBY SILVER CO. QUADRUPLE PLATE" and anchor over a crown mark. Circa 1890.

889. STERLING SILVER. Marked with a tiny (1/8"high) fleur-de-lis in a shield and "STERLING 15." Possibly Davis & Galt of Philadelphia, Pa. Circa 1900.

890. SILVERPLATE. Marked "HOMAN SILVERPLATE CO. QUADRUPLE PLATE." Circa 1896. Same as #784.

891. SILVERPLATE. Marked "PAIRPOINT MFG. CO. NEW BEDFORD, MASS. QUADRUPLE PLATE, 1925" and "P" in a diamond mark. Ads refer to "Bright cut" incised design. The cost was "plain, $1.75; bright cut $2.00; gold lined 25 cents extra." Also see #872. Ref: PMCC illustration lacks design.

892. SILVERPLATE. Marked "BARBOUR SILVER CO. SILVER, QUADRUPLE 2184." Circa 1892.

893. SILVERPLATE. Figural. Marked "MERIDEN SILVERPLATE CO. QUADRUPLE PLATE, 079." 2" high. Circa 1890.

894. SILVERPLATE. Marked "NEW HAVEN SILVER PLATE CO. QUADRUPLE PLATE, 079." Incised with "TOOTHPICKS". Circa 1891.

895. STERLING SILVER. Hallmarked with "G" "S" anchor in a shield, lion passant in a shield, and lower case letter "g" in a shield. This means it was made in Birmingham, England in 1906. 2 1/4" high.

896. SILVERPLATE. Marked "PAIRPOINT MFG. CO. NEW BEDFORD, MASS., QUADRUPLE PLATE, 1928", with "P" in a diamond mark. 2 3/4" high. Circa 1894. Ref: PMCC without the engraving.

897. SILVERPLATE. Marked "MERIDEN B CO., QUADRUPLE PLATE, C2" and "186" with balance scale mark. Circa 1890.

898. SILVERPLATE. Applied band. Marked "FORBES SILVER CO., QUADRUPLE 588" with bird mark. Circa 1894.

899. SILVERPLATE. Marked "APOLLO SILVER CO., QUADRUPLE PLATE, 383" with fleur-de-lis mark. Circa 1899.

900. SILVERPLATE. Marked "PAIRPOINT MFG. CO., NEW BEDFORD, MASS., QUADRUPLE PLATE, 1937" with "P" in a diamond mark. Circa 1894. Ref: PMCC.

901. SILVERPLATE. Marked "BARBOUR SILVER CO., SILVER, QUADRUPLE, 25." Circa 1892.

902. SILVERPLATE. Marked "PAIRPOINT MFG. CO., NEW BEDFORD, MASS., QUADRUPLE PLATE, B3723." Probably early 1900's.

903. SILVERPLATE. Marked "FORBES SILVER CO., QUADRUPLE 206" with eagle mark. Circa 1894.

904. SILVERPLATE. Star and web mark, plus "PAT. APPLIED FOR 448." Made by E.G. Webster & Son, Brooklyn, N.Y., circa 1896.

905. SILVERPLATE. Marked "HOMAN MFG. CO. N.Y., MADE IN USA, 286, SPECIAL METAL" and anchor with entwined rope, shovel and pail. Circa 1900.

906. SILVERPLATE. Marked "MERIDEN S P 75." Circa 1898.

907. SILVERPLATE. Marked "STEVENS SILVER CO., PORTLAND, MAINE, QUADRUPLE PLATE, 185" with an iron cross mark. It reads "TAKE YOUR PICK." Circa late 1890's.

908. SILVERPLATE. Marked "REED & BARTON, SILVER SOLDERED. 2 1/2, CHAUNCEY WRIGHT. " Possibly had a glass liner.

909. SILVERPLATE. Marked "FORBES SILVER CO., QUADRUPLE PLATE, 574" with eagle mark. Embossed rim. Circa 1894.

910. SILVERPLATE. Maker and age unknown.

911. SILVERPLATE. Marked "MANHATTAN SILVER PLATE CO., QUADRUPLE PLATE, 926" with crescent and star mark. 2 1/4" tall. Circa 1890.

912. SILVERPLATE. Marked "PAT. JUN 14, 1904, B. VICTOR SILVER CO., QUADRUPLE PLATE, 1537." A Derby Silver Co. mark on less expensive items. Circa 1904.

913. SILVERPLATE. Marked "JAMES W. TUFTS, BOSTON, MASS., 3469." It reads "DESTROYED BATTLESHIP MAINE, FEBRUARY 15, 1898" above the steamship. 2 1/2" high.

914. SILVERPLATE. Marked "WILCOX SILVER PLATE CO., QUADRUPLE PLATE, MERIDEN, CONN., GILT, 6112" with crossed hammers mark. 2 1/2" high. Circa 1890.

915. SILVERPLATE. Marked "PAIRPOINT MFG. CO., NEW BEDFORD, MASS., QUADRUPLE PLATE" with "P" in a diamond mark. Rim design is open, flower is incised. 2 1/4" high.

916. SILVERPLATE. Marked "DERBY SILVER CO., QUADRUPLE PLATE, 1736, HIGH GRADE METAL" with anchor over a crown mark. Applied embossed openwork rim. Circa 1890.

917. SILVERPLATE. Marked "MONARCH SILVER CO., QUADRUPLE PLATE, 23" with star over a crown mark. Also marked "HIGH GRADE METAL" with an arm holding a hammer. Made by Knickerbocker Manufacturing Co., circa 1904.

918. SILVERPLATE. Marked "DERBY SILVER CO., QUADRUPLE PLATE, 1735, HIGH GRADE METAL" with anchor over a crown mark. Circa 1890.

919. SILVERPLATE. Marked "MERIDEN B COMPANY, QUADRUPLE PLATE, 58, USA" with a shield and balance scales mark. Center part includes leaves, vines, three birds with open wings and three lion heads. Circa 1890.

920. SILVERPLATE. Made by Hartford Silver Plate Co., circa 1896. Flat-chased design.

921. SILVERPLATE. Marked with a "W" inside a star and a web around it, and "318, QUADRUPLE PLATE." Made by E.G. Webster & Son. A frog (hidden) sitting at the base and a salamander are applied. It is incised "TAKE YOUR PICK."

922. SILVERPLATE. Marked "THE VAN BERGH S.P. CO., ROCHESTER, N.Y., QUAD PLATE, 866." Circa 1900.

923. SILVERPLATE. Marked "PAIRPOINT MFG. CO., PAT. APPLIED FOR, 3713." Same as #767. Ref: PMCC states "Patented Aug. 22, 1893."

924. SILVERPLATE. Marked "Derby Silver Co; Derby, Conn." and "1730." Weighted bottom, anchor mark. Circa 1890.

925. SILVERPLATE. Marked "DERBY SILVER CO., QUADRUPLE PLATE, 1753" over a crown mark. Circa 1890.

926. SILVERPLATE. Marked "VAN BERGH SILVER PLATE CO., QUAD PLATE, ROCHESTER, N.Y., 961." Circa 1904.

927. SILVERPLATE. Marked "COLONIAL SILVER CO., QUADRUPLE PLATE, PORTLAND, MAINE, X, OK." Circa 1900's.

928. SILVERPLATE. Marked "F.B. ROGERS SILVER CO., TAUNTON, MA., QUADRUPLE PLATE, 1524" with crown mark. 2 3/8" high. Circa 1890.

929. SILVERPLATE. Marked with "322" and a star with a "W" inside and a web around it. Made by E.G. Webster & Son. Circa 1900.

930. SILVERPLATE. Marked "POOLE SILVER CO., QUADRUPLE PLATE, TAUNTON, MA.,53." Circa 1893.

931. SILVERPLATE. Marked with "QUADRUPLE PLATE" over an "R". Rising Sun mark in a circle with an "R" in the center. Made by Bernard Rice's Sons, circa 1904. Souvenired "KANSAS CITY." Ref: R-EASM.

932. ALUMINUM. Tumble-up. Reads "NIAGARA FALLS."

933. ALUMINUM. Tumble-up.

934. ALUMINUM. Tumble-up, possibly anodized to darken. Incised, the inscription probably reads "PAN AMERICAN EXPO 1901."

935. ALUMINUM. Pedestal toothpick holder or drinking glass.

936. ALUMINUM. Tumble-up. Incised "World's Fair St. Louis 1904."

937. ALUMINUM. Tumble-up. Incised "WASHINGTON, D.C." with a red and blue shield.

938. ALUMINUM. Tumble-up with incised design around the edge. Anodized to black.

939. ALUMINUM. Tumble-up with embossed design around edge.

940. ALUMINUM AND GLASS. Top part screws on. When the bottom is heavy enough, it will tumble up. Clear and milk glass. In another version, there is a narrow Greek Key design between two rows of beads in the top portion of the glass.

941. ALUMINUM. Tumble-up.

942. ALUMINUM. Incised "PICKS."

943. ALUMINUM. Incised "NIAGARA FALLS."

944. PRESSED GLASS, clear. Wrap-around brass trim. 2 3/4" high. Back side shows a flower; front side shows a nude woman. Probably foreign. Possibly Art Deco.

945. HIGH HANDLED HEXAGON. Heavy silver overlay. Possibly Westmoreland Glass Co., circa 1910. Ref: H-R/U #1260.

946. PRESSED GLASS. Milk glass with metal filagree. Probably early 1900's. Maker unknown.

947. ONE-O-ONE. Challinor & Taylor, circa 1890's. Blue opaque with metal filagree. Ref: H-1 #187.

948. VICTORIA, FOSTORIA'S. Fostoria Glass Co., circa 1888-1890. Clear with filagree. Ref: H-R/U #1168.

949. GLASS. Clear with silver band around the top. Possibly Val St. Lambert. Circa 1905-1910. Ref: H-R/U #1085 is same shape and size.

950. PRESSED GLASS. Clear with twisted wires locked into metal base. Maker and date unknown.

951. PRESSED GLASS. Clear with silver overlay of grapes on the center panels and flowers on the other four panels. Possibly European of recent vintage.

952. PRESSED GLASS. Clear with silver overlay showing buildings on three panels and a scroll design on other panels. Age and maker unknown.

953. INTAGLIO VINE AND FLOWER (NBW). Erroneously called Daisy & Bluebell in NTHCS *Toothpick Bulletin*, January/February, 1989. Intaglio portion decorated with silver or platinum. Maker still unknown.

954. TWO SIZE PANEL (NBW). Maker unknown. Alternate panels are of different widths. Silver overlay design. Also known in black glass.

955. CO-OP'S RAY aka NINE PANEL COLONIAL. Cooperative Flint Glass, circa 1900-1920. Heavy silver overlay. Ref: H-R/U #1248.

956. FLUTE. Imperial Glass Co. Made in carnival marigold over clear, carnival marigold over light vaseline, carnival green, carnival amethyst, and clear. Seldom found with silver deposit trim.

Note: This pattern also attributed to Northwood, whether marked or not, particularly when the top rim is less rounded and has sharper edges. Sometime after 1950, Imperial issued this FLUTE with a similarly squared top rim edge in clear and in amber with a foil sticker resembling a coin on each panel. It sold as a cigarette holder. Ref: H-l #119-121.

957. CHIPPENDALE aka COLONIAL NIGHTS. Originally by Jefferson and Central Glass. Found with cuttings as well as with silver deposit. Ref: H-1000 #775.

958. DAISY & BUTTON. Clear with metal. This is also known in amber with a similar lattice overlay. Ref: H-1 #89.

959. CURVY SANITARY (NBW). Silver overlay. Possibly foreign. May be 1930's-1940's or later.

960. VIGILANT. Fostoria Glass Co. #403. Clear with silver deposit. Ref: H-R/U #1175.

961. HOLLY, PEDESTALLED. Indiana Tumbler and Goblet Co. of Greentown, Indiana. Circa 1902-1903. Also found in a swirled amber opalescent color, called HOLLY AMBER. Both are extremely rare. This is only known example in clear glass. Ref: H-1000 back cover for Holly Amber.

962. THREE IN ONE aka FANCY DIAMONDS. Imperial Glass Co. #1. Rim flares on this circa 1902 holder. Reissued in 1960's and 1970's with straight sides in several translucent colors, iridized colors and slag glass. Old one is known in clear only. Ref: H-1000 #592 for reissue.

963. INTERLOCKED HEARTS aka WISHBONE. Maker unknown. Probably circa 1890's. Ref: K-VOL V and W-PG page 252.

964. RIBBED DRAPE. Jefferson Glass Co. #250. Made after 1907. Clear, custard, apple green, and electric blue. Usually decorated. Ref: H-1, #250 and #251.

965. WREATH & SHELL aka Manila (OMN). Model Flint Glass Co. at Albany, Indiana, circa 1901. Made in clear and opalescent colors of white, blue and canary. This one is decorated with gold. Ref: H-1 #329-331.

966. WESTON. Robinson Glass Co. #123 at Zanesville, Ohio. Circa 1895. Note difference in flare on top and sides when compared to #967. Easily confused with RETORT. See NTHCS *Toothpick Bulletin*, October, 1980, and H-R/U #1195.

967. WESTON. Same as #966, but it has a wider opening due to hand finishing.

968. ORINOCO. A.J. Beatty Co., circa 1888. Ref: MC-EPG.

969. THREE FRUITS. Jenkins Glass Co. #860. Circa 1920's. Same as #983. Ref: B-AG and H-JJ (indexed as Fruit Salad).

970. STIPPLED FORGET-ME-NOT (WITH FLOWERS). Kamm credits two companies with this pattern: Bryce Brothers in Pittsburgh during the 1880's, and Model Flint Glass at Findlay, Ohio after 1891. Model Flint moved to Albany, Indiana in 1893. Many shards were found at the Findlay Flint Glass (1889-1891) factory site, but not at either Model location according to Smith. Only clear reported to date, but blue, white or amber could have been made. Shards of some items without flowers have been found. Beware of items with ground tops. Ref: K-IV and S-FPG.

971. PANELLED SPRIG. Northwood Glass Co., circa 1898. Made in clear, cranberry, milk glass, rubina, apple green, amethyst, and white opalescent. Frequently decorated and sometimes stencil etched. Ref: H-1 #203 and #289; H-1000 #194; and HMW-NOR.

972. POINTED GOTHIC. Indiana Glass Co. #453 with frosted panels. Circa 1920's-1930's. Ref: H-1000 #602.

973. COLONIAL STAIRSTEPS. Possibly H. Northwood and Co. Circa 1906. Made in clear and light blue opalescent. The opalesence may be at the top or the bottom. Recent research by James Measell has not confirmed Northwood as the maker. Ref: H-2. Also see 239.

974. DAISY & BUTTON. Hobbs, Brockunier & Co. from 1885. Made in clear, old gold stained, sapphire blue, apple green, canary, and amberina. Ref: H-1 #72, #78 and #79.

975. ALEXIS. Fostoria Glass Co., circa 1910. Clear only. Reproduced in pink, yellow and blue in 1980's for the Fostoria Glass Society. Brass stand. The same stand is also found in silverplate. Six-sided recess in the metal stand is obviously for this particular toothpick holder. Ref: H-1000 #661.

976. PURITAN. McKee Glass Co., circa 1915-1920. Known only in clear. Ref: H-1000 page 99.

977. LEAF & STAR. New Martinsville Glass Co., circa 1909. Found in clear, ruby stain, marigold stain, deep amber and cobalt blue. This one has good gold trim. Ref: H-1000 #852.

978. QUILT (OMN) aka FLORETTE and BULGING PETALS. Consolidated Lamp & Glass Co., Fostoria, Ohio, circa 1885. Known in pink, mauve, bright green, three shades of blue, yellow, white, red satin, pigeon blood, apricot stain and clear. Colors may be mixed with white. They may be frosted or shiny and/or cased. FLORETTE is a similar pattern known only in salt shakers. The FLORETTE flowers look flatter and more diamond shaped. Also see #64. Ref: H-1 #'s 112-115; Pioneer, newsletter of the Antique and Art Glass Salt Shaker Collectors Assn.

979. ATLAS. Applied ornate metal band on top and at base. Found in clear, milk white, and ruby stained. Also found with a beaded top in milk glass, a previously unlisted variation. Ref: H-1000 #223.

980. MCKEE COLONIAL (#20). Circa 1910-1920. Known only in clear and clear with color stain. Item shown is souvenired. Ref: H-1000 page 99.

981. NEVADA. U.S. Glass Co. #15075. Known in clear, ruby stain and with floral decoration. Ref: H-1000 #864.

982. ROYAL IVY. Northwood Glass Co. Circa 1890. Shown here frosted with clear leaves and vines. Produced in shiny and frosted colors of clear, rubina, cased spatter, craquelle, and white. Very rare in amber stain and clambroth white. Ref: H-1 #262-266.

983. THREE FRUITS. Jenkins Glass Co. #860. Circa 1920's. Same as #969. Ref: B-AG and H-JJ (indexed as Fruit Salad).

984. DECO DRAPE. Czechoslovakian. Circa 1920's. Shown here in clear with gold panels and top. Also known in deep amethyst. Ref: H-R/U #1348.

985. KINGFISHER. Original made by Canton Glass Co., circa 1890-1899. To distinguish the old from the new, examine the base at the point where the tails of two fish overlap. On the old, the tail of the fish on the right is above the tail of the other fish in each pairing. On newer items, the positions of the tails are reversed on one of these pairings. Ref: H-R/U page 86; GB-ON, p. 29.

986. KINGFISHER. St. Clair reproduction. Made in many colors, some iridized. Within the last few years, someone is using yet another mold.

987. EARLY TAPERED BLOCK HAT (NBW). This is the old hat. Attributed to both Iowa City Glass and Fostoria Glass Co., and could have been made by both. One example found with "W.V. Rieger, 802 Main St., Kansas City" embossed on the brim. Generally of poor quality, thick glass, the type commonly attributed to Iowa City. Heacock's H-1000, #199, is widely found in many colors and was made by Kemple Glass. Also see #370. Ref: R-IC.

988. PANAMA. U.S. Glass Co. #15088. Differs from the referenced one in that the base is recessed. This may be the second shape Heacock mentions, or one may be a shot glass. Circa 1898-1910. Ref: H-1000 #841.

989. CONNECTICUT. U.S. Glass Co. #15068, circa early 1900's. Several U.S. Glass patterns used this stenciled decoration. Ref: H-R/U #1190.

990. U.S. FLUTES (NBW). This has the entwined "U S G" (U.S. Glass Co.) logo in the bottom. Probably circa 1915.

991. VENECIA. Heacock attributed it to either Consolidated or West Virginia Glass Co., circa 1885-1890. Colors include clear (shown here with gold trim), milk, decorated milk, cranberry, rubina, light green fading to clear, pigeon blood, ruby and green. Ref: H-1000 #123, #137 and #195.

992. YUTEC. McKee Glass Co. Probably circa 1909-1920. Like several late McKee toothpick holders, this was probably made by hand shaping the top of a whiskey tumbler (shot glass). Ref: S-MK.

993. COLONIAL BELLE. Now known to have been made by Lancaster Glass Co., circa 1910. Wire cut flower pattern. Ref: H-R/U #1249.

994. LOUISIANA. U.S. Glass Co., circa 1890. Most probably a mustard pot and originally had a lid.

995-996. ZANESVILLE. Robinson Glass Co. of Zanesville, Ohio, circa 1900. Two variations of frosted glass with enameled flower decoration. The difference in size and shape is due to hand finishing.

997. COLONIAL TWIN. Maker unknown. Six scallops and six wide panels. Ref: H-R/U #1247.

998. PEDESTALLED PANEL WITH LENS (NBW). Unidentified. Characteristic of a pattern of the 1860's, before toothpick holders.

999. COLUMBIA aka OLD COLUMBIA. Columbia Glass Co. of Findlay, Ohio, circa 1891. Known only in clear. Ref: HR/U page 88; MS-FG pages 33-34.

1000. PLACID. New Martinsville Glass Co., circa 1906. This shape was also made with thumbprints about 1908 and is known as PLACID THUMBPRINT. Ref: H-R/U #1183.

1001. FROSTED SHELLS (NBW). Maker unknown. Three shells have been added to this blown spittoon shaped item. May be a small vase.

1002. TEA ROOM. Made by Indiana Glass Co., 1926-1931. Mustard jar without a lid. Made in pink, green, amber and clear. Ref: F-CEDG.

1003. PREPAREDNESS. Circa 1917. See *American Historical Glass* by Bessie M. Lindsay, pp. 487-9.

1004. FLARED PANELS (NBW). Shape strongly resembles Riverside's #550 aka WINSOME H-1000 #616. Similar star under base, but unlike WINSOME, foot is plain. Maker and date unknown.

1005. COLONIAL MYSTERY (NBW). Another plain paneled holder. Eight sides, sixteen point star in the base. Known in clear and black. Shown here with a cut decoration. Maker and date unknown.

1006. LEAFY SCROLL. U.S. Glass Co. #15034, circa 1896. Clear only. Ref: H-5 page 172; K-IV page 91; and MC-EPG.

1007. PURITAN, TARENTUM'S. Looks like LADDERS without the notches. Ref: W-PG.

1008. FLUTE. Imperial Glass Co. See #956. Top flare will vary due to hand finishing. Ref: H-1 #119-121.

1009. STUDIO. New Martinsville Glass Co. #721. Circa 1910. Made only in clear, sometimes decorated. Shown here with green stained leaves. Ref: M-NM.

1010-1011. ANTHONY & DIANA. Intaglio images frosted. Holder slightly oval in shape. Possibly European. Only other item known in this pattern is a small, shallow nut dish or ash tray.

1012. STUDIO. See #1009 above. This one has gold on the leaves.

1013. FERN WITH LILY OF THE VALLEY. Tentative attribution, a match holder circa mid-1800's. Probably European.

1014. IVY, SANDWICH. Attributed to Boston & Sandwich Glass Co. Probably a match holder, circa 1840's. Ref: H-1 #159.

1015. INGROWN TOES (NBW). Maker and age unknown. Purplish tint. Known in poorly done ruby stain. Recently produced by Smith Glass in clear and clear iridized, but with legs that turn out instead of inward. Research continues.

1016. SCROLLED SHELL. Circa 1896. Known in clear, milk glass and decorated milk glass. Shown here in clear with goofus-like paint. Ref: H-1000 #394.

1017. FRENCH PANELS (NBW). Possibly Baccarat. This style is typically continental, popular in France and Belgium for many years. The glass has a pink tinge and features alternating panels of fine overshot glass and gold trim. Other colors and decorations are probable. Also see #287. Ref: H-R/U page 93, #602.

1018. FRENCH SWIRLS (NBW). St. Louis Glass, circa 1900. Brilliant glass with swirls running from top to bottom. Every other rib striated. The bottom also has a swirl pattern. Ref: H-R/U page 93 #605.

1019. ALMOST CUT (NBW). Unidentified. Could be a bar glass.

1020. CRYSTAL OVALS (NBW). Probably recent lead crystal with gold decoration, possibly from Germany. The base is ground and the glass and decoration are of very good quality.

1021. LENOIR. New Martinsville Glass Co. #715, circa 1911. Panels with three vertical grooves alternate with plain panels. Ref: M-NM.

1022. LACY FLORAL. Westmoreland Specialty Glass Co., circa 1904. Panels alternate with similar but slightly different flowers. One flower has six petals, the other has eleven. Known only in clear. Ref: Mc-EPG. (Note: This reference's attribution of a similar pattern, BEADED FLOWER, to Indiana Tumbler & Goblet Co. is considered to be an error.)

1023. REX aka FANCY CUT. Cooperative Flint Glass Co., circa 1904. This shape is the toothpick holder. Heacock's earlier reference pictured the toy spooner. Ref: H-1000 #719 (toy spooner).

1024. HEART IN SAND. New Martinsville Glass Co. #724, circa 1908. Known in clear and clear with ruby stain. Ref: H-1000 page 100.

1025. INDIAN HEAD MATCH HOLDER. This one is believed to be old since there is a fiery translucence to the glass. Gold decoration is typical of about 1915. Sometimes found with divider across center to separate used from unused matches. Widely reproduced by Kemple in nearly all colors and sometimes marked with "K". Ref: W-MG.

1026. LEAF & PLEAT. Pittsburgh Brass & Lamp (Dithridge), circa 1906-1907. Two pieces. Known in clear frosted and white milk glass. The top part is known in blue milk glass, but no pedestal seen to date. Set is a miniature jardinere. Ref: H-R/U #1222; H-1000 #360.

1027. DOLPHINS WITH SEASHELLS (NBW). Looks like Vallerystahl, however Westmoreland made other items in this pattern which they called NAUTILUS. Research continues. Ref: M-TP, Plate xxx.

1028. BULLDOG MATCH SAFE. McKee Glass Co., circa 1899. Ref: F-YMG.

1029. FLARED ROUND PANELS (NBW). Milk glass. Maker unknown. Research continues.

1030. SHELLWARE. Alton Manufacturing Co., 1907-1909. Milk Glass. Ref: NTHCS *Toothpick Bulletin*, April, 1988.

1031. SHELLWARE. See #1030 above. Note scroll design around the top rim that is lacking on the one above.

1032. CLOUD BAND. Gillinder & Sons, circa 1880's. A toy spooner which is 2 3/8" in diameter. (Toy sugar is 2 15/16" in diameter.) Ref: L-TG.

1033. NO BEES (NBW). Milk glass. This is identical to BEES IN A BASKET, except there are no bees. Ref: H-R/U #1352-1354.

1034. LOOP-FOOTED. Called KNOTTY PINE in the November, 1984 NTHCS *Toothpick Bulletin*. Ref: W-MG.

1035. FLEUR DE LIS AND FERN (NBW). Milk glass. Age and maker unknown. Research continues.

1036. KEYSTONE. McKee Glass Co., circa 1897. Found in clear, etched clear, milk glass and light custard with goofus gold. Ref: H-1000 #615.

1037. SHELLS & FLOWERS (NBW). Note the little flowers around the rim of this unidentified item. Age and maker unknown.

1038-1039. TRAMP'S SHOE (Right and Left). Circa 1890. Maker unknown. Difficult to find the pair with matching decoration. Reproduced in many colors by Degenhart. Ref: H-1000 #390.

1040. THREE FLOWERS (NBW). Often found as a souvenir item, mounted in a seashell holder with plaster.

1041. SUNDEW (NBD). Maker unknown. Circa 1906-1915. 2 5/8" tall.

1042. SUMBA (NBD). Maker unknown. Circa 1910-1925. 2 5/8" tall. Square solid base with step cut corners. Possibly Czech.

1043. SWALLOW (NBD). Maker unknown. Circa 1915-1925. 2 5/8" tall. Cross hatching on each panel identifies this as a later item. Seven scallops form the rim.

1044. CLYDESDALE (NBD). Maker unknown. Circa 1905-1915. 2 3/4" tall. Cut star in base. Three large pyramidal stars with cross cut diamonds on body.

1045. McBROOM (NBD). Maker unknown. Circa 1910-1920. 2 1/2" tall. Eight panels with a girdle middle.

1046. FOUR CORNERS (NBD). Maker unknown. Circa 1910-1920. 2 1/2" tall. Solid base with cross-cut diamond and fans. Also found with a cut star replaces the cross-cut diamonds in two panels.

1047. JO ANN (NBD). Probably made by Pitkin and Brooks, based on the yellow color of the blank. Circa 1915-1925. 2 1/2" tall. Paperweight base of St. Louis diamond and notched prism. Cross-cut diamonds over a plain lozenge on top half of holder.

1048. PATTON (NBD). Probably made by J. Hoare & Co., circa 1895-1906. 2 5/8" tall. Sixteen point star under base. Body has eight point star in a cross-hatched background, with fans. Ref: B-ABCG page 161.

1049. LEVI (NBD). Maker unknown. Circa 1900-1910. 2 1/2" tall. Pedestal base cut with St. Louis diamond. Cross hatching triangles around the body.

1050. CROSBY (NBD). Probably made by J. Hoare & Co., circa 1905-1915. 2 1/2" tall. Star under base. Notched top, crossed ellipticals around body. Ref: FS-COR page 44.

1051. COWPOKE (NBD). Maker unknown. Circa 1915-1925. 2 3/4" tall. Solid base cut in Harvard pattern. Four panels alternate cut star and cut fan motifs.

1052. PAULA (NBD). Maker unknown. Circa 1905-1915. 2" tall. Solid base of notched prism. Body of St. Louis diamonds. Stars and fans around top.

1053. MABEL (NBD). Marked "MAPLE CITY GLASS CO." Circa 1900-1912. 3 3/8" tall. Pedestal with ball in stem. Cut star under base. Notched rim. Body cut with fan with cross, diamond and hobnail in a diamond field.

1054. JEWEL (NBD). Probably made by C.F. Monroe. Circa 1905-1916. Pedestal with ball in stem. Cut star under base. Notched rim. Body of almond shaped ovals and St. Louis diamond.

1055. SABLE (NBD). Maker unknown. Circa 1910-1920. 3 1/4" tall. Cut star under base. Body has ball cut with punty bullseyes and cross-cut diamonds around top.

1056. MINK (NBD). Probably made by J. Hoare & Co., circa 1890-1906. 3 1/4" tall. Pedestal with ball stem. Cut star under base. Notched rim. Body cut in pinwheel and boxed star. Ref: S-CEG page 292.

1057. GRAVIC CARNATION (OMN). Marked T.G. Hawkes & Co., circa 1906-1915. 3 1/4" tall. Cut star under base. Notched rim. Body has grey cut (unpolished) carnations. Ref: R-CEG page 184.

1058. SARATOGA (OMN). Probably made by M.G. Averbeck Manufacturer, circa 1892-1920. 3" tall. Pedestal with cut star under base. Body is cut in the buzz-star pattern. Ref: E-CG page 56.

1059. JUDGE (NBD). Marked "T. G. HAWKES & CO." Circa 1910-1915. 3 1/4" tall. Pedestal with cut star under base. Body of boxed stars and boxed fans. Top of straight cut flutes. Ref: FS-COR page 96.

1060. RADIUM (OMN). Probably made by M.J. Averbeck, circa 1900-1910. 3 1/4" tall. Pedestal with cut star under base. Body of expanding stars and fans over diamond filled with cross hatching. Notched rim. Ref: E-CG page 32.

1061. THISTLE (OMN). Probably made by T.B. Clark & Co., circa 1910-1925. 3 1/4" tall. Pedestal with cut star under base. Body has three large cut thistles with leaves and stems. Ref: S-CEG page 252.

1062. ST. BERNARD (NBD). Marked "LIBBEY GLASS CO.", circa 1910-1925. 2 1/2" tall. Cut star under footed base. Zipper cuts on all eight panels. Body has chain of diamonds with crossed lines.

1063. DELFT DIAMOND (OMN). Possibly made by T.G. Hawkes & Co., circa 1920-1930. Some are marked. 2 7/8" tall. Footed base. Body has Delft diamond and a ring of cross cut diamond with X cuts.

1064. STAR FEATHER (OMN). Marked "LIBBEY GLASS CO.", circa 1906-1920. 2 5/8" tall. Cut star under base. Body has flashed stars and flashed feather. Ref: F-LG page 301.

1065. HOPE (NBD). Maker unknown. Circa 1905-1910. Late brilliant cut type. 2 3/8" tall. Notched thumbprint top. Three large hobstars in a diamond field around the body. Twelve point star cut in base.

1066. BOYD (NBD). Maker unknown. Circa 1905-1910. Late brilliant cut type. 2 1/4" tall. Plain hobnail square with handles.

1067. ADA (NBD). Maker unknown. Circa 1905-1910. Late brilliant cut type. 2 1/4" tall. Fan and strawberry diamond pattern.

1068. LOTTO (NBD). Marked Libbey Glass Co. Circa 1910-1920. Late brilliant cut type. 2 1/4" tall. Thumbprint around top. Body has hobstar in a diamond field, then a fan in a diamond. Ref: F-LG page 301 #1025.

1069. DEE DEE (NBD). Maker unknown. Circa 1910-1920. 2 1/8" tall. Raised hobstar with straight line cuts.

1070. SUN DOG (NBD). Possibly made by J.D. Bergen Co. based on sunburst cut. Circa 1910-1915. 2 1/4" tall. Sunburst with notched rays. Clear thumbprint in center.

1071. COLONIAL (OMN). Made by C. Dorflinger & Sons. Circa 1893-1910. 2 1/2" tall. Cut fans rim, cut star in base.

Very busy pattern. Patented by James O'Connor, July 4, 1893. Ref: F-AFG pages 112, 114.

1072. ODD (OMN). Marked T.G. Hawkes Co. Circa 1900-1906. 2 1/2" tall. Horizontal step cutting under a fan. Hobstar in a diamond field above X cut vesica (pointed oval). Ref: FS-COR page 91.

1073. VAL (NBD). Marked Libbey Glass Co. Circa 1910-1925. 2 1/2" tall. Star cut under base. Body has double crosscut diamonds, bullseye panel and fan panels. Also see #1164. Ref: F-LG page 301.

1074. LOCKPORT (NBD). Marked Libbey Glass Co. Circa 1915-1925. 2 1/4" tall. Bottom half is hobnail with raised bottom. Later cut.

1075. SUNSPOT (NBD). Maker unknown. Circa 1900-1915. 7/8" tall. Two large sunbursts with plain centers and notched prisms between.

1076. PEG LEGS (NBD). Maker unknown. Circa 1895-1910. 2 3/8" tall. Three legs. Large hobstar next to a large fan around the body. Very rare.

1077. WEBER (NBD). Marked Webb Corbett (England). Circa 1910-1930. 2 5/8" tall. Chain of V-cut connected flutes.

1078. GOPPY (NBD). Maker unknown. Circa 1900-1915. 2" tall. Fans on top and bottom. Four large notched hobnails.

1079. FOLIAGE (NBD). Maker unknown. Circa 1910-1925. 2 1/2" tall. Notched rim and foot. Stem and leaves wind around the bulbous body.

1080. ERWIN (NBD). Maker unknown. Circa 1910-1925. 2 5/8" tall. Sixteen point star under base. Flute cuts.

1081. MANSFIELD (NBD). Maker unknown. Circa 1906-1915. 2 1/2" tall. Sixteen point star under base. Cut flowers with vine and leaves.

1082. PRISMATIC (NBD). Probably made by Quaker City Cut Glass Co. Circa 1902-1924. 2" tall. Fourteen columns of notched prism. Polished base. Ref: QCCG page 84.

1083. DOROTHY (NBD). Maker unknown. Circa 1906-1920. 2 1/4" tall. Scalloped rim with eight clear flute panels at top. Chain of stars and strawberry diamonds around base.

1084. DUNCAN (NBD). Maker unknown. Circa 1910-1925. 2 1/4" tall. Side notched flutes at top. Four thumbprints around the body with stars between thumbprints.

1085. CICERO (NBD). Probably made by Pitkin and Brooks. Circa 1915-1920. 2 1/2" tall. Thick, heavy base with a nailhead diamond cut. Cut flowers and leaves on top half. Shown in 1917 catalog. Ref: E-CGPG page 39.

1086. SNOWFLAKE (NBD). Libbey Glass Co., circa 1915-1925. 2 1/4" tall. Cut in square checkerboard with big clear crossed bars. Ref: F-LG page 231.

1087. CHESS BOARD (NBD). Maker unknown. Circa 1900-1910. 1" tall, 4" long. Sanitary lay-down type. Cut in cane (aka Chairbottom or Hobnail) and cross.

1088. COYOTE (NBD). Maker unknown. Circa 1910-1920. 2" tall. Notched vertical flutes that are hollowed out, broken up by straight horizontal line cuts.

1089. MARBLE (NBD). Probably made by Pitkin and Brooks. Circa 1900-1920. 2 5/8" tall. Solid ball base of strawberry diamonds. Top of plain notched panels. Ref: M-NO plate IV.

1090. SPIDER (NBD). Probably made by Pitkin and Brooks. Circa 1910-1930. 2 3/8" tall. Body is miter and prism. Ref: E-CG page 28.

1091. MARCO (NBD). Maker unknown. Circa 1900-1915. 2 3/8" tall. Good quality cut, notched bottom rim. Body is chain of hobstar and fan design.

1092. BART (NBD). Maker unknown. Circa 1915-1925. 2 3/8" tall. Body is large triangles of straight crossed lines between long stemmed fans.

1093. MOON SIGN (NBD). Probably made by J.D. Bergen Co. 1905-1920. 2 1/4" tall. Notched prism columns, bullseyes, flashed stars and cross-cut squares. Ref: E-CG page 127.

1094. KARMA (NBD). Maker unknown. Circa 1900-1915. 2 1/4" tall. Unusual shape and cut. Large hob stars.

1095. LANDWIND (NBD). Made by J.D. Bergen Co., circa 1915-1925. 2 1/4" tall. Notched prism columns with single cuts on alternating panels. Polished base.

1096. BIRCH (NBD). Maker unknown. Circa 1910-1925. 2 1/2" tall. Unusual shape with cross-cut diamond on bottom. Horizontal step cutting around a twisted body.

1097. NEWGATE (NBD). Maker unknown. Circa 1910-1925. 2 5/8" tall. Zipper cut on each edge of each of seven panels. Chain of hobstars around bottom.

1098. LAURA (NBD). Made by Cambridge Glass Co., pattern #4019. Circa 1910-1916. 2 1/4" tall. Ten panels, cut flowers, leaves and vines. Polished base. Ref: W-CG I page 110.

1099. BUTTERFLY HUMMINGBIRD (NBD). Maker unknown. Circa 1915-1930. 2 1/2" tall. Steel cut hummingbird on one side, butterfly on the other.

1100. FLORIST (NBD). Maker unknown. Circa 1910-1925. 2 1/2" tall. Polished base. Notched prism on each corner. Six petal flower with stem and leaves on all four sides.

1101. HEATHER (NBD). Probably made by Pitkin & Brooks. Circa 1915-1925. 2 3/8" tall. Square shape, vertical column with zipper cut only in the middle. Ref: S-CEG page 113; M-NO (match holder, circa 1900).

1102. LILITH (NBD). Marked as made by Libbey, but may be fake. Circa 1915-1925. 2 1/4" tall. Six petal flowers around the body with stems and leaves.

1103. PILGRIM (OMN). Possibly C.F. Monroe Co. Circa 1900-1916. 2" tall. Eight panels with two gangcuts around the body. Eight point star cut under base. Ref: M-CCG page 13.

1104. PINSTAR (NBD). Maker unknown. Imported, probably European. Circa 1900-1915. 2 1/4" tall. Pinwheel front and back. Ref: E-CGPG catalog reprint.

1105. STARDUST (NBD). Maker unknown. Circa 1905-1920. 2 1/4" tall. Notched prism with a hobstar in a diamond field.

1106. DOVER (NBD). Maker unknown. Circa 1910-1925. 2 1/4" tall. English hobnail and fan. May be a mustard or a cigarette holder.

1107. GLACIER (NBD). Maker unknown. Circa 1895-1905. 2 1/4" tall. Strawberry diamond and fan.

1108. McLAIN (NBD). Maker unknown. Circa 1905-1915. 2" tall. Notched prism column, lozenges, and a large strawberry diamond.

1109. WATER FLOWER (NBD). Maker unknown. Circa 1910-1925. 2 3/8" tall. Flashed flower with stem. May not be a toothpick holder.

1110. ST. LOUIE (NBD). Maker unknown. Circa 1910-1920. 2 1/2" tall. St. Louis diamond (also called honeycomb) all over.

1111. JUNE (NBD). Maker unknown. Circa 1910-1920. 2 1/4" tall. Notched rim. Six petal flower around body.

1112. SUN DANCE (NBD). Maker unknown. Circa 1910-1920. 2 3/8" tall. Eight petal, large well cut flower. Flat rim and size indicate possibly a mustard without lid.

1113. LORD CORK (NBD). Marked Waterford. Circa 1950-1970. 2 1/2" tall. Relief diamonds.

1114. ROYAL BOHEMIAN (NBD). Made in Bohemia. Circa 1913-1925. 2 1/4" tall. Hobstars in diamond field with fans on all four sides. Ref: H-PGP Issue #1.

1115. WEST SLAVIC (NBD). Made in Bohemia. Circa 1910-1916. 2" tall. Two large X cuts, with fans above and below, separating two large hobstars. Ref: H-PGP Issue #1.

1116. SERBIA (NBD). Made in Bohemia. Circa 1910-1916. 2 1/2" tall. Side notched rim. Fan and hobstar in a diamond field. Ref: E-CGPG page 7.

1117. SUGAR CANE (NBD). Maker unknown. Circa 1900-1915. 1 7/8" tall. Pattern is called cane, chairbottom or hobnail and cross.

1118. TWIN CITIES (NBD). Maker unknown. Circa 1910-1920. 2 1/2" tall. Four double vertical column zipper cuts with cross cut squares in the middle of the columns.

1119. CZECH (NBD). Made in Bohemia. Circa 1910-1915. 2" tall. Pinwheels and notched prisms. Ref: H-PGP Issue #1.

1120. MIDDLE SILESIA (NBD). Made in Bohemia. Circa 1910-1915. 2 1/4" tall. Hobstar in triangle alternating with large fan designs. Ref: H-PGP Issue #1.

1121. COMANCH (NBD). Maker unknown. Circa 1910-1925. 2 1/4" tall. Twelve notched vertical columns with cross cut squares in the middle of the columns.

1122. SILESIA (NBD). Made in Bohemia. Circa 1910-1915. 2 1/8" tall. Hobstar in a triangle, then a large fan design. Ref: H-PGP Issue #1.

1123. MORAVIA (NBD). Made in Bohemia. Circa 1910-1915. 2 1/4" tall. Sixteen notched prism columns. Also known in 2" toothpick holder. Ref: H-PGP Issue #1.

1124. CZECHOSLOVAKIA (NBD). Made in Bohemia. Circa 1910-1915. 2 3/8" tall. Pinwheel and notched prism columns. Ref: H-PGP Issue #1.

1125. AMES (NBD). Maker unknown. Circa 1905-1915. 2 5/8" tall. Pedestal base with side cuts. Fans with nailhead diamond panels.

1126. WALLY (NBD). Maker unknown. Circa 1910-1920. 2 1/4" tall. Polished base. Straight cut across the middle of X cuts.

1127. DELINDA (NBD). Maker unknown. Circa 1906-1920. 2 3/8" tall. Intaglio cut poppy flowers with stems and leaves. Possibly a ground down shaker. Ref: W-CG II page 110 #1209.

1128. INDIES (NBD). Maker unknown. Circa 1910-1920. 2 1/2" tall. Square shape. Fans cut on corners and on top of the cross hatched pyramid.

1129. LEE (NBD). Maker unknown. Circa 1905-1915. 2 1/4" tall. Round body has two large flashed pinwheels.

1130. MAYPOLE (NBD). Maker unknown. Circa 1910-1930. 2" tall. Six panels, double cut X over and under a split six sided diamond.

1131. PATRON (NBD). Maker unknown. Circa 1900-1915. 2 1/2" tall. Cut star under base. Fans and hobstar in a diamond field on body.

1132. DIVINE (NBD). Maker unknown. Circa 1910-1920. 2 3/8" tall. Twelve columns of vertical notched prism that extend to form a notched rim.

1133. DEW DROPS (NBD). Maker unknown. Circa 1910-1920. 2 1/4" tall. Four wide pillars of wave like scallops extend down to become feet. Four notched panels between.

1134. GENESIS (NBD). Maker unknown. Circa 1910-1920. 2" tall. Eight plain panels, no cutting. Polished base. May be an uncut blank.

1135. PAGE (NBD). Maker unknown. Circa 1915-1930. 2" tall. Plain uncut bottom. Vertical cut all around the top portion. The middle is nailhead diamonds.

1136. FAIRBORN (NBD). Maker unknown. Circa 1915-1925. 2 1/2" tall. No cutting, but nice shape. Three large vertical triangular columns separated by two smaller columns. Also known with notched edges.

1137. ROBIN (NBD). Maker unknown. Circa 1895-1910. 2" tall. Fifteen point star under base. Crossed ellipticals with fan.

1138. LAFAYETTE (NBD). Made by Taylor Bros. Circa 1902-1910. Not marked. 2 3/8" tall. Deep (1/2") solid base. Alternating columns of notched prism and plain prism. Ref: T-CCG.

1139. THISTLE ROSE (NBD). Made by Cambridge Glass Co. Circa 1910-1920. 2 5/8" tall. Paperweight base. Cut thistle three times around the body. Ref: W-CG II page 110.

1140. MICHAEL (NBD). Maker unknown. Circa 1910-1920. 2 1/2" tall. Collar-like foot. Uneven notched rim. Plain panels with a chain of cross cut star around the bottom.

1141. TAPERED TIFFIN (NBK). Made by U.S. Glass Co. Circa 1914. 2 3/8" tall. Sharp cut. Notched corners. Cross cuts with fans. Ref: H-R/U page 91; B-TG III page 17.

1142. TAPERED TIFFIN (NBK) (Pressed). Made by Tiffin Glass Co. Circa 1920-1935. 2 3/8" tall. Same pattern as above, but no cutting.

1143. RACHEL (NBD). Maker unknown. Circa 1900-1915. 2 1/8" tall. Nailhead diamond, split by notched prism and cross cuts.

1144. SARAH TIFFIN (NBD). Made by Tiffin Glass Co. Circa 1914. One is known with a paper label. 2 3/8" tall. Notched prism column, cut only in the middle. Ref: H-R/U page 91; B-TG I I I page 17.

1145. POOTER (NBD). Maker unknown. Circa 1910-1925. 2 1/4" tall. Deep notched solid base. Six panels with six pointed stars around the top. Possibly Czech. Also shown as #1167.

1146. POLLY (NBD). Maker unknown. Circa 1910-1930. 2 3/8" tall. Notched rim and base. Ring of gang cuts around body.

1147. CAPRICORN DAISY (NBD). Maker unknown. Circa 1910-1920. 2 1/2" tall. Paperweight base. Six petal cut flower.

1148. CANE BOTTOM (NBD). Maker unknown. Circa 1900-1920. 2" tall. Notched prism column next to chairbottom panels.

1149. DAISY TRIO (NBD). Maker unknown. Circa 1910-1930. 2 1/2" tall. Three long stemmed daisy-like flowers.

1150. STOCKHOLM (NBD). Marked Orrefors Glass Co., Sweden. Circa after World War I. 2 1/2" tall. Lead crystal glass with art deco style butterfly. Orrefors still makes cut glass items.

1151. PANDA (NBD). Circa 1905-1915. 2 1/2" tall. Intaglio cutting of flowers, stems and leaves left a silvery gray. Possibly a Cambridge Glass Co. mustard. Shaker in Cambridge pattern #1035 known with this design. Ref: W-CG II page 110.

1152. NOBLE (NBD). Marked "MADE IN CZECHO-SLOVAKIA." Circa 1910-1930. 2" tall. Thick, good quality glass. Straight, deep cuts.

1153. PAGODA (NBD). Maker unknown. Circa 1915-1930. 2 1/2" tall. Good quality glass. Eight panels with little or no cutting.

1154. NUTMEG (NBD). Maker unknown. Circa 1915-1930. 2 1/2" tall. Eight panels that interlock in the middle give this a very nice shape. No cutting.

1155. MERCURY (NBD). Maker unknown. Circa 1915-1930. 2" tall. Plain polished lead crystal.

1156. ELENA (NBD). Maker unknown. Circa 1915-1930. 2 1/8" tall. Eight deep V cuts around the body. Base cut into nine large hobnails. Very unusual.

1157. QUARTZ (NBD). Maker unknown. Circa 1915-1930. 2 1/2" tall. Eight plain panels. Lead crystal.

1158. UNIONTOWN (NBD). Maker unknown. Circa 1906-1925. 2 1/2" tall. Intaglio cut thistles, flowers with stem and leaves left unpolished.

1159. THOR (NBD). Maker unknown. Circa 1915-1925. 2 1/2" tall. Rim is side notched. Flared body has flashed pinwheels.

1160. ANNE (NBD). Maker unknown. Circa 1906-1925. 2 1/2" tall. Eight panels with intaglio cut flowers, stems and leaves left unpolished.

1161. GINGER (NBD). Maker unknown. Circa 1900-1920. 3 1/2" tall. Pedestal with ball stem. Fifteen point star under base. Body has diamond of cross cut diamond and strawberry diamonds. Ref: M-BB.

1162. MEBANE (NBD). Possibly made by Pitkin and Brooks. Circa 1900-1910. 3" tall. Fans cut on corners of rim. Body has diamonds of cross cut diamonds and field of cross cut squares. Sixteen point star under the base. Ref: M-NO plate IV.

1163. TERRY (NBD). Maker was Irish or English. Silver rim has British Sterling mark. Circa 1910-1930. 2 1/2" tall. Flat footed base. Fans, diamond stars and cross cut squares around the body.

1164. VAL (NBD). Marked Libbey Glass Co. Circa 1910-1925. 2 1/2" tall. Star cut under base. Body has double cross cut diamonds, bullseye panel and fan panels. Ref: F-LG page 301.

1165. CANFIELD (NBD). Maker unknown. Circa 1900-1915. 2" tall. Round body of chairbottom (aka Cane or Hobnail) and cross.

1166. HENRY (NBD). Maker unknown. Circa 1900-1920. 2 1/2" tall. Side cuts on foot. Panels of steps under a fan, separated by panels of cross cut diamonds.

1167. POOTER (NBD). See #1145.

1168. LUCY (NBD). Maker unknown. Circa 1915-1930. 2" tall. Blue tint and spots in bottom. Flower, vine and leaves. Rim is turned in.

1169. ELBE (NBD). Marked Czechoslovakia. Circa after World War II. 2 1/4" tall. Green rectangular shape. Four corners have horizontal steps. Middle has vertical columns between column of raised plain diamonds.

1170. LEAH (NBD). Maker unknown. Circa 1920-1940. 2 1/2" tall. Pink. Rim is side notched. Body has raised diamonds. Base has flat thumbprint cuts.

1171. PURPLE MARTIN (NBD). Maker unknown. Circa 1900-1910. 2 1/2" tall. Brass rim. Amethyst or purple cut glass. Fan over star in a diamond, and cross cut diamond.

1172. BUTTON ARCHES. Ruby stain, souvenired. Duncan Miller Glass Co., Washington, Pa., circa 1914. Pattern introduced in 1885 by George Duncan Co. and is still produced by other companies. Ref: H-1 #42.

1173. ROYAL IVY. Frosted rubina. The Northwood Glass Co., circa early 1890's. Made in many Northwood colors. Ref: H-1 #262-266; HMW-NOR.

1174. WILLIAM R. HEACOCK COMMEMORATIVE TOOTHPICK HOLDER. Fenton Art Glass, 1991. Limited edition made for NTHCS 1991 convention. Burmese glass with photo decal of Heacock. Shape is like Madoline (aka Swinger in Ref: H-1000) pattern originally produced by Cooperative Flint Glass Co. about 1890. See also 259.

SILVERPLATE FIGURALS

698 699 700 701

702 703 704 705

706 707 708 709

87

SILVERPLATE FIGURALS

710   711   712   713

714   715   716   717

718   719   720   721

SILVERPLATE FIGURALS

SILVERPLATE FIGURALS

SILVERPLATE

STERLING SILVER, SILVERPLATE & PEWTER

SILVERPLATE FIGURALS

SILVERPLATE FIGURALS

SILVERPLATE FIGURALS

SILVERPLATE

SILVERPLATE FIGURALS

METAL FIGURALS

SILVERPLATE AND OTHER METALS

848 849 850 851

852 853 854 855

856 857 858 859

SILVERPLATE AND OTHER METALS

SILVERPLATE

SILVERPLATE AND STERLING SILVER

884   885   886   887

888   889   890   891

892   893   894   895

SILVERPLATE

SILVERPLATE

908 909 910 911

912 913 914 915

916 917 918 919

SILVERPLATE

105

ALUMINUM

106

OVERLAY AND DEPOSIT TRIM

107

BLOWN AND PRESSED GLASS

961 962 963 964

965 966 967 968

969 970 971 972

BLOWN AND PRESSED GLASS

973   974   975   976

977   978   979   980

981   982   983   984

BLOWN AND PRESSED GLASS

PRESSED GLASS

MILK GLASS

113

CUT GLASS

1041   1042   1043   1044

1045   1046   1047   1048

1049   1050   1051   1052

CUT GLASS

CUT GLASS

1065 1066 1067 1068
1069 1070 1071 1072
1073 1074 1075 1076

CUT GLASS

CUT GLASS

1089

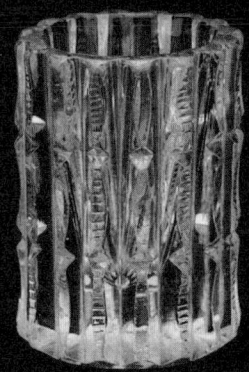
1090

1091

1092

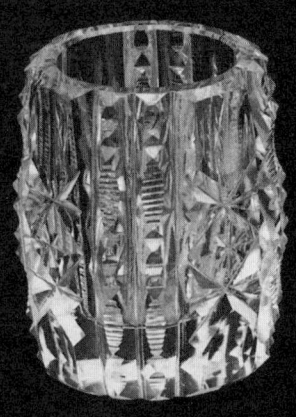
1093

1094

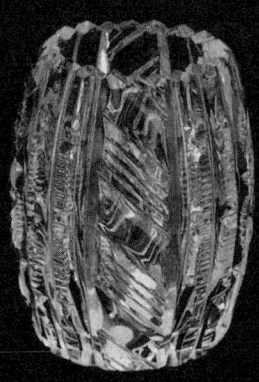
1095

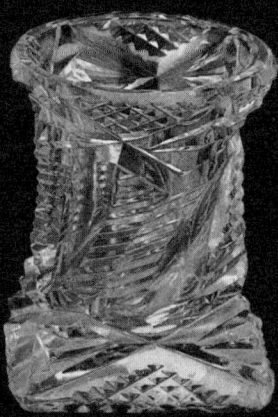
1096

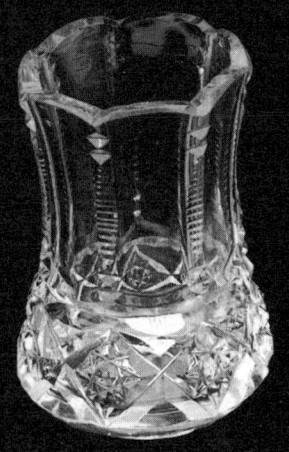
1097

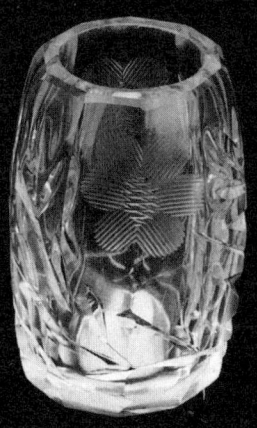
1098

1099

1100

CUT GLASS

1101　　1102　　1103　　1104

1105　　1106　　1107　　1108

1109　　1110　　1111　　1112

CUT GLASS

CUT GLASS

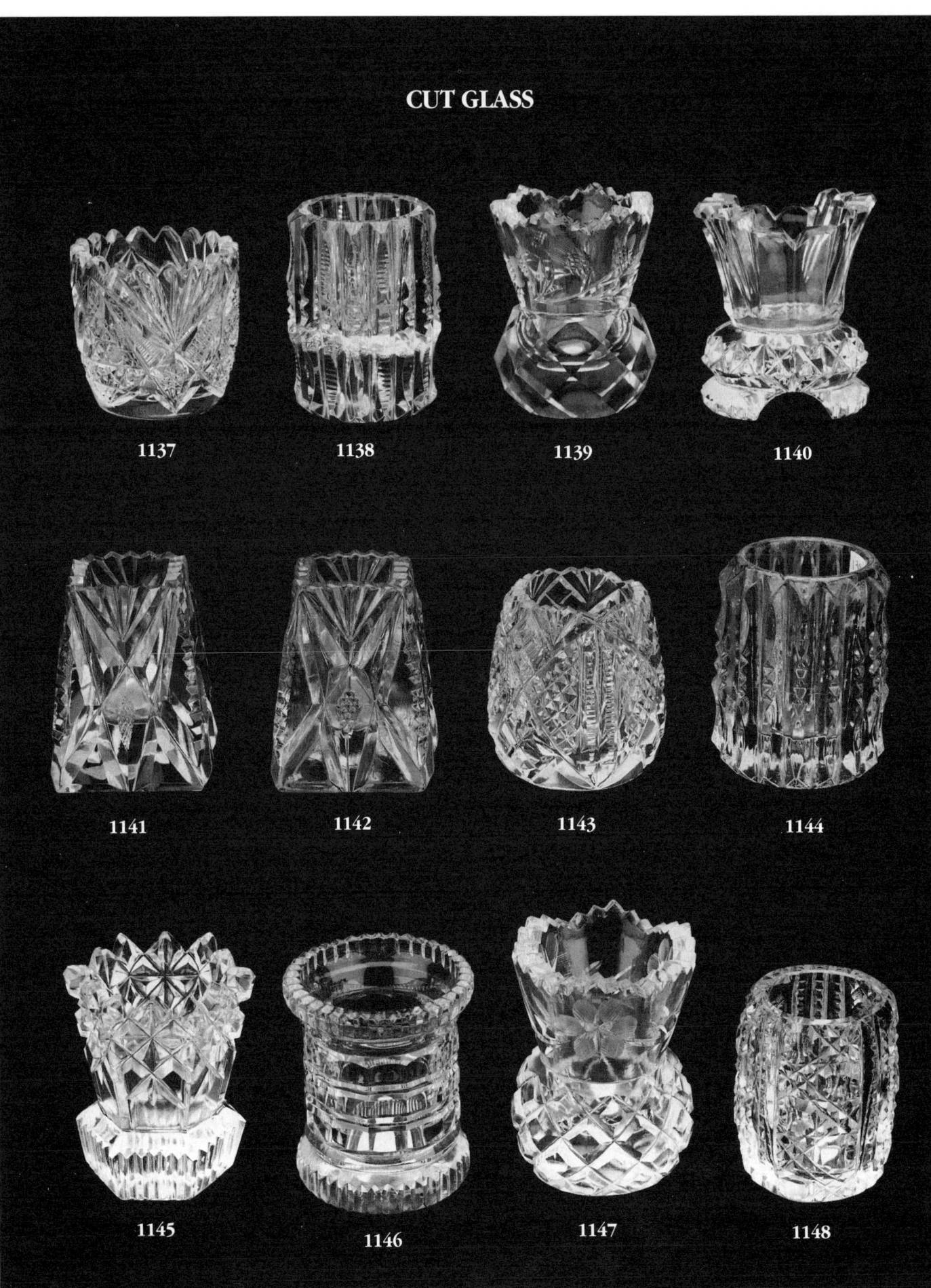

CUT GLASS

1137　1138　1139　1140
1141　1142　1143　1144
1145　1146　1147　1148

CUT GLASS

1149　1150　1151　1152

1153　1154　1155　1156

1157　1158　1159　1160

CUT GLASS

BIBLIOGRAPHY

Key

B-PP	Bagdade, Susan and Al. *English & Continental Pottery & Porcelain.* Willow Grove, PA: Warman, 1987.
BC-AG	Baldwin, Gary and Carno, Lee. *Moser - Artistry in Glass 1857-1938.* Marietta: Antique Publications, 1988.
BK-GIS	Barlow, Raymond E. and Kaiser, Joan. *The Glass Industry in Sandwich,* Vol II. Barlow-Kaiser Pub Co. Inc. & Schiffer Pub Ltd., 1989.
B-MG	Belknap, E.M. *Milk Glass.* New York: Crown, 1949.
B-TG I	Bickenheuser, Fred. *Tiffin Glassmasters.* Grove City, OH: by author, 1979.
B-TG II	Bickenheuser, Fred. *Tiffin Glassmasters, Book II.* Grove City, OH: by author, 1981.
B-TG III	Bickenheuser, Fred. *Tiffin Glassmasters, Book III.* Grove City, OH: by author, 1985.
B-CCG	Blackmer, A. L. Co., *Catalog of Cut Glass 1906-1907* (reprinted by ACGA, 1982).
B-ABCG	Boggess, Bill and Louise. *Identifying American Brilliant Cut Glass.* New York: Crown, 1984.
B-AG	Bond, Marcelle. *The Beauty of Albany Glass.* Berne, IN: by author, 1972.
BOUL-TP	Boultinghouse, Mark. *Art and Colored Glass Toothpick Holders.* N.p.: 1966.
BFM-DUN	Bredehoft, Neila M., Fogg, George A. and Maloney, Francis C. *Early Duncan Glassware.* N.p.: by authors, 1987.
CG-C	Cambridge Glass Co., *1903 Catalog of Pressed and Blown Glass Ware.* (reprinted by NCC, Inc., 1976).
C-CFM	Cohen, Wilfred R. *Wavecrest - The Glass of C. F. Monroe.* Paducah: Collector Books, 1987.
E-CCG	Egginton, O. F. Co. *Catalog of Cut Glass Circa 1910.* Published by ACGA, 1982).
E-CGPG	Ehrhardt, Alpha. *Cut Glass Price Guide.* Kansas City, MO: Heart of America, 1973.
EW-BG	Eige, Eason and Wilson, Rick. *Blenko Glass 1930-1953.* Marietta: Antique Publications, 1987.
EA-CC	Eikelberner, George and Agadjanian, Serge. *American Glass Candy Containers.* Belle Mead, NJ: by authors, 1967.
ECG-CCG	Empire Cut Glass Co. *Catalog of Cut Glass.* (Reproduced by ACGA, 1980).
E-CG	Evers, Jo. *The Standard Cut Glass Value Guide.* Paducah: Collector Books, 1981.

FS-COC	Farrar, Estelle and Spillman, Jane. *The Complete Cut & Engraved Glass of Corning.* New York: Crown, 1979.
F-LG	Fauster, Carl. *Libbey Glass Since 1818.* Toledo: Len Beach Press, 1978.
F-AFG	Feller, John. *Dorflinger - America's Finest Glass.* Marietta: Antique Publications, 1988.
F-YMG	Ferson, Regis F. and Mary F. *Yesterday's Milk Glass Today.* Pittsburgh: by authors, 1981.
F-CEDG	Florence, Gene. *The Collector's Encyclopedia of Depression Glass.* Paducah: Collector Books, 1984.
F-MC	Forsythe, Ruth A. *Made In Czechoslovakia.* Galena, OH: by author, 1982.
G-GC	Galpin, John. *Handbook of Goss China.* 1972. Portsmouth, England: by author, 1972.
G-RS 1	Gaston, Mary Frank. *The Collector's Encyclopedia of R. S. Prussia.* Paducah: Collector Books, 1982.
G-RS 2	Gaston, Mary Frank. *The Collector's Encyclopedia of R. S. Prussia,* Second Series. Paducah: Collector Books, 1986.
GCD	*Glass Collectors Digest,* various issues, 1987-1991.
G-BPPM	Godden, Geoffrey. *Encyclopedia of British Pottery and Porcelain Marks.* New York: Crown, 1964.
GB-ON	Griscom, Pauline and Boyd, Helen. *Is It Old? Is It New?* N.p.: 1988.
G-AGN	Grover, Ray & Lee. *Art Glass Nouveau.* First edition. C. E. Tuttle, 1967.
H-PGP	Heacock, William. *Pattern Glass Preview.* Various issues.
H-GC	Heacock, William. *The Glass Collector.* Various issues.
H-CG	Heacock, William. *Collecting Glass.* Various issues.
H-1	Heacock, William. *Toothpick Holders from A to Z.* Marietta: Antique Publications, 1974; second edition, 1976.
H-2	Heacock, William. *Opalescent Glass from A to Z.* Marietta: Antique Publications, 1975; second edition, 1977.
H-3	Heacock, William. *Custard Glass from A to Z.* Marietta: Antique Publications, 1976.
H-4	Heacock, William. *Syrups, Sugar Shakers & Cruets from A to Z.* Marietta: Antique Publications, 1976.
H-1000	Heacock, William. *1000 Toothpick Holders.* Marietta: Antique Publications, 1977.
H-5	Heacock, William and Bickenheuser, Fred. *U. S. Glass from A to Z.* Marietta: Antique Publications, 1978.
H-FEN 2	Heacock, William. *Fenton Glass The Second Twenty-Five Years.* O-VAL Advertising Corp. 1980.

H-6	Heacock, William. *Oil Cruets from A to Z.* Marietta: Antique Publications, 1981.
H-OPG	Heacock, William. *Old Pattern Glass According to Heacock.* Marietta: Antique Publications, 1981.
HJ-S	Heacock, William and Johnson, Patricia. *5000 Open Salts.* Marietta: Antique Publications, 1982.
H-R/U	Heacock, William. *Rare & Unlisted Toothpick Holders.* Marietta: Antique Publications, 1984.
H-7	Heacock, William. *Ruby-Stained Glass from A to Z.* Marietta: Antique Publications, 1986.
H-9	Heacock, William and Gamble, William. *Cranberry Opalescent Glass from A to Z.* Marietta: Antique Publications, 1987.
HMW-NOR	Heacock, William; Measell, James; and Wiggins, Berry. *Harry Northwood: The Early Years 1881-1900.* Marietta: Antique Publications, 1991.
H-JJ	Hicks, Joyce Ann. *Just Jenkins.* Kokomo, IN: by author, 1988.
HU-WEL	Huxford, Sharon and Bob. *The Collectors Encyclopedia of Weller Pottery.* Paducah: Collector Books, 1979.
J-HTP	Jones, Nancy and David. *Heisey Toothpick Holders.* Newark, OH: Heisey Collectors of America, 1982.
J-CPB	Jones-North, Jacquelyne Y. *Czechoslovakian Perfume Bottles and Boudoir Accessories.* Marietta: Antique Publications, 1990.
K-VOL	Kamm, Minnie Watson. *Pattern Glass Pitchers.* Vols. I-VIII. Grosse Pointe, MI: by author, 1939-1954.
K-LCT	Koch, Robert. *Louis C. Tiffany, Rebel in Glass.* New York: Crown, 1964.
K-TAG	Koch, Robert. *Tiffany's Art Glass.* New York: Crown, 1977.
K-NDM	Kovel, Ralph and Terry. *Kovel's New Dictionary of Marks.* New York: Crown, 1986.
L-DCF	Lechler, Doris Anderson. *Children's Glass Dishes, China and Furniture.* Paducah: Collector Books, 1983.
L-DCF II	Lechler, Doris Anderson. *Children's Glass Dishes, China and Furniture* Vol. II. Paducah: Collector Books, 1986.
L-TG	Lechler, Doris Anderson. *Toy Glass.* Marietta: Antique Publications, 1989.
LCH-SAL1	Lechner, Ralph and Mildred. *The World of Salt Shakers.* Paducah: Collector Books, 1976.
LCH-SAL2	Lechner, Ralph and Mildred. *The World of Salt Shakers,* second edition. Paducah: Collector Books, 1992.
L-VG	Lee, Ruth Webb. *Victorian Glass.* Framingham Centre, MA: by author, 1944.

L-EAPG	Lee, Ruth Webb. *Early American Pressed Glass.* Northboro, MA: by author, 1946.
L-SG	Lee, Ruth Webb. *Sandwich Glass.* Wellesley Hills, MA: by author, 1947.
L-AG	Lee, Ruth Webb. *Nineteenth-Century Art Glass.* New York: Barrows, 1952.
L-USM	Lehner, Lois. Lehner's *Encyclopedia of U. S. Marks on Pottery, Porcelain & Clay.* Paducah: Collector Books, 1988.
L-PGS	Luckey, Carl F. *Official Price Guide to Silver-Silverplate.* Florence, AL: House of Collectibles, 1978.
MC-EPG	McCain, Molly. *The Collector's Encyclopedia of Pattern Glass.* Paducah: Collector Books, 1982.
M-GG	Measell, James. *Greentown Glass.* Grand Rapids: Grand Rapids Public Museum. 1979.
MS-FG	Measell, James and Smith, Don E. *Findlay Glass: The Glass Tableware Manufacturers, 1886-1902.* Marietta: Antique Publications, 1986.
M-NO	Mebane, John. *What's New That's Old.* N.p.: Barnes, 1970.
M-BB	Mebane, John. *Collecting Brides' Baskets and Other Glass Fancies.* Des Moines: Wallace-Homestead, 1976.
M-EAPG	Metz, A. H. *Early American Pattern Glass* Vol. I. Paducah: Collector Books, 1958.
M-TP	Mighell, Florence. *A Collectors Book on Toothpick Holders.* Des Moines: Wallace-Homestead, 1973.
MM-PGPG	Miles, Dori and Miller, Robert W. (eds.). *Price Guide to Pattern Glass.* Lombard, IL: Wallace-Homestead, 1986.
M-OG	Millard, S. T. *Opaque Glass.* Topeka: Central Press, 1941.
M-NM	Miller, Everett & Addie. *The New Martinsville Glass Story.* Marietta: Richardson Publishing Co. 1972.
M-MG	Miller, Robert W. *Mary Gregory and Her Glass.* Des Moines: Wallace-Homestead, 1972.
M-CCG	Monroe, C. F. Co., *Catalog of Cut Glass.* (Reproduced by ACGA, N.d.).
M-GC	Moody, C.W. *Gouda Ceramics.* N.p.: by author, 1970.
NTHCS-B	National Toothpick Holder Collectors Society *Toothpick Bulletin,* various issues 1980-1991.
OL-LAG	O'Connor, D. Thomas and Lotton, Charles G. *Lotton Art Glass.* Marietta: Antique Publications, 1990.
PMCC	*Pairpoint Manufacturing Co. 1894 Catalog Reprint.* Washington Mills, NY: Gilded Age Press, 1979.
P-CCG	Parsche, F. X. & Son Co. *Catalog of Cut Glass.* (Reproduced by ACGA, 1981).

P-GSS	Peterson, Arthur G. *Glass Salt Shakers.* Des Moines: Wallace-Homestead, 1970.
P-GPP	Peterson, Arthur G. *Glass Patents and Patterns.* Sanford, FL: by author, 1973.
QCCG	Quaker City Cut Glass Co. *Catalog of Cut Glass.* (Reprinted by ACGA, N.d.).
R-ASP	Rainwater, Dorothy T. and H. Ivan. *American Silverplate.* West Chester, PA. Schiffer, 1988
R-EASM	Rainwater, Dorothy T. *Encyclopedia of American Silver Manufacturers.* West Chester, PA: Schiffer, 1986.
RH-CE	Random House. *Collector's Encyclopedia: Victorian and Art Deco.* New York: Random House, 1974.
R-l9CG	Revi, Albert Christian. *Nineteenth Century Glass.* New York: Thomas Nelson & Sons, 1959.
R-CEG	Revi, Albert Christian. *American Cut & Engraved Glass.* New York: N.p., 1965.
R-CBA	Revi, Albert Christian (ed.). *The Spinning Wheel's Complete Book of Antiques.* New York: Grosset & Dunlap, 1972.
R-IC	Righter, Miriam. *Iowa City Glass.* Des Moines: Wallace-Homestead, 1966.
S-NAP	Schnadig, Victor K. *American Victorian Figural Napkin Rings.* Des Moines: Wallace-Homestead, 1971.
S-CPW	Selman, L. H. *Collector's Paperweights.* Santa Cruz, CA: L. H. Selman Ltd. Paperweight Press, 1983.
S-AAG	Shuman, John A, III. *The Collector's Encyclopedia of American Art Glass.* Paducah: Collector Books, 1988.
S-FPG	Smith, Don E. *Findlay Pattern Glass.* Findlay, OH: Courier Commercial, 1970.
S-GT	Spillman, Jane Shadel. *Glass Tableware, Bowls and Vases.* New York: Knopf, 1982.
S-MK	Stout, Sandra McPhee. *The Complete Book of McKee Glass.* North Kansas City, MO: Trojan, 1972.
S-CEG	Swan, Martha Louise. *American Cut and Engraved Glass.*
T-CCG	Taylor Bros. & Co. *Catalog of Cut Glass.* (Reprinted by ACGA, N.d.).
T-RSP	Terrell, George W. Jr. *Collecting R. S. Prussia.* Florence, AL: Books Americana, 1982.
V-NIP	Van Patten, Joan F. *The Collector's Encyclopedia of Nippon Porcelain.* Paducah: Collector Books, 1979.
V-NIP 2	Van Patten, Joan F. *The Collector's Encyclopedia of Nippon Porcelain, Second Series.* Paducah: Collector Books, 1982.

V-NIP 3	Van Patten, Joan F. *The Collector's Encyclopedia of Nippon Porcelain,* Third Series. Paducah: Collector Books, 1986.
V-NOR	Van Patten, Joan F. *The Collector's Encyclopedia of Noritake.* Paducah: Collector Books, 1984.
W-HH	Waher, Bettye. *The Hawkes Hunter: T. G. Hawkes, 1880-1962.* N.p., by author.
W-MG	Warman, Edwin G. *Milk Glass Addenda.* Uniontown, PA: by author, 1966.
W-ACG	Warman, Edwin G. *American Cut Glass.* Uniontown, PA: by author, 1978.
WP-W	Warner, Ian and Posgay, Mike. *The World of Wade.* Marietta: Antique Publications, 1988.
W-PG	Welker, John and Elizabeth. *Pressed Glass in America: Encyclopedia of The First Hundred Years, 1825-1925.* Ivyland, PA: by authors, 1985.
W-CG	Welker, Mary, Lyle & Lynn (eds.). *The Cambridge Glass Co.* Vols. I & II (A reprint of parts of old company catalogs). New Concord, OH: N.p., 1970.
W-CD	Whitmyer, Margaret & Ken. *Children's Dishes.* Paducah: Collector Books, 1984.
Y-SG	Yalom, Libby. *Shoes of Glass.* Marietta: Antique Publications, 1988.

INDEX

A
Acme Silver Co. 71
Ada (1067) 82 Illustrated 116
Agata (146-7) 5 Illustrated 26
Alexander (267) 9 Illustrated 33
Alexandrite (83, 138) 3, 5 Illustrated 22, 25
Alexis, Dalzell's (263) 9 Illustrated 33
Alexis, Fostoria's (975) 78 Illustrated 109
Alligator (340) 11 Illustrated 38
Almost Cut (1019) 80 Illustrated 112
Alton Mfg. Co. 81
Aluminum xii, 77
Amana (390) 13 Illustrated 41
Amberina (4, 79-82, 84-6, 88, 91) 1, 3 Illustrated 17, 22
American Beauty Rose (124) 4 Illustrated 24
Ames (1125) 84 Illustrated 121
Anne (1160) 85 Illustrated 123
Anthony (1010) 80 Illustrated 111
Apollo Silver Co. 76
Arizona (269) 9 Illustrated 34
Art Deco 10-1
Art Glass xiv, 1-7
Atlas (979) 79 Illustrated 109
Aurora Jewels (368) 12 Illustrated 40
Aurora Silverplate 1, 3, 71-2, 74-5
Aurora, Northwood's (66, 105) 3, 4 Illustrated 21, 23
Averbeck, M.J. 82

B
Babcock & Co. 1, 70
Baby Mine (358) 12 Illustrated 39
Barbour Silver Co. 70, 76
Barrel (153-5) 5 Illustrated 26
Bart (1092) 83 Illustrated 118
Bead Rim Basket (363) 12 Illustrated 39
Beaded Flower 80
Beaded Grape (271) 9 Illustrated 34
Beaded Panel & Sunburst (279) 9 Illustrated 34
Bearded Man with Staff (350) 11 Illustrated 39
Beaty Co., A.J. 78
Beaumont Glass 8
Bees in a Basket 81
Beggars Hand (356) 12 Illustrated 39
Bellaire Goblet Co. 11
Belmont Glass Co. 12
Benedict Mfg. Co. 74
Bergen Co. 82
Bergen Co. 83
Birch (1096) 83 Illustrated 118
Bird in Stump (339) 11 Illustrated 38
Bisque 66, 68-9
Blue Opaque (205) v, 7 Illustrated Front Cover, 30
Bluina (7) 1 Illustrated 17
Boston & Sandwich Glass Co. 5, 80
Boyd (1066) 82 Illustrated 116
Brazil 13
Brenner Bros. Co. 75
Brenner-Hall (395) 14 Illustrated 41
Brilliant (255) 8 Illustrated 33
Bristol (308, 311, 377) 10, 13 Illustrated 36, 40
Bryce Bros. 1, 11, 78
Buckingham (268) 9 Illustrated 34
Bulb Base (115, 134) 4, 5 Illustrated 24-5
Bulbous Ring Neck (66, 105) 3, 4 Illustrated 21, 23
Bulge Base (326, 343) 11 Illustrated 37-8
Bulging Petals (64, 978) 2, 79 Illustrated 21, 109
Bulldog Match (1028) 81 Illustrated 113
Burmese (6, 9, 10, 17-27, 29, 109, 117, 207-8, 210, 212) 1, 4, 7 Illustrated 17-8, 24, 30
Burmese, Simulated (28, 45) 1, 2 Illustrated 18-9
Butler Bros. 11, 61
Butterfly Hummingbird (1099) 83 Illustrated 118
Button Arches (1172) vi, 86 Illustrated Back Cover

C
California (271) 9 Illustrated 34
Cambridge Glass Co. 83-5
Cameo Glass (14, 158, 161, 170) 1, 5 Illustrated 17, 27
Cane Bottom (1148) 85 Illustrated 122
Canfield (1165) 85 Illustrated 124
Canton Glass Co. 79
Capricorn Daisy (1147) 85 Illustrated 122
Cat Toothpick (334) 11 Illustrated 38
Cat on a Pillow (334) 11 Illustrated 38
Challinor & Taylor 12, 77
Cherry Thumbprints (389) 13 Illustrated 41
Cherubs (353) 12 Illustrated 39
Chess Board (1087) 83 Illustrated 117
China v, xiii, xiv, 14-6, 61, 65-70
Chippendale (957) 78 Illustrated 107
Cicero (1085) 82 Illustrated 117
Clark & Co. 82
Cloisonne (228, 233-4) 7 Illustrated 31
Cloud Band (1032) 81 Illustrated 113
Clydesdale (1044) 81 Illustrated 114
Co-op's Ray (955) 78 Illustrated 107
Co-op's Royal (225) 7 Illustrated 31
Colonial (1071) 82 Illustrated 116
Colonial Belle (993) 79 Illustrated 110
Colonial Mystery (1005) 80 Illustrated 111
Colonial Nights (957) 78 Illustrated 107
Colonial Silver Co. 77
Colonial Stairsteps (239, 973) 7, 78 Illustrated 32, 109
Colonial Twin (997) 79 Illustrated 111
Colonial, Indiana's (264) 9 Illustrated 33
Columbia (999) 79 Illustrated 111
Columbia Glass Co. 79
Columned Thumbprints (246) 8 Illustrated 32
Comanch (1121) 84 Illustrated 120
Connecticut (989) 79 Illustrated 110
Consolidated Lamp & Glass 2, 3, 9, 10, 79
Contemporary Art Glass 6, 7, 29, 30
Coolie (351) 12 Illustrated 39
Cooperative Flint Glass Co. vi, 7, 8, 11, 77, 80, 86
Coralene (12, 135) 1, 5 Illustrated 17, 25
Cowpoke (1051) 81 Illustrated 114
Coyote (1088) 83 Illustrated 117
Crackle Glass (328) Illustrated 37
Crider, Terry 6, 7, 13-4
Criss-Cross (102) 4 Illustrated 23
Crocodile (340) 11 Illustrated 38
Crocodile Tears (71-3) 3 Illustrated 21
Crosby (1050) 81 Illustrated 114
Crowned Flowers (303) 10 Illustrated 36
Crystal Ovals (1020) 80 Illustrated 112
Curtain Top Overlay (120) 4 Illustrated 24
Curvy Sanitary (959) 78 Illustrated 107
Cut Block (252) 8 Illustrated 32
Cut Glass xv, 10, 11, 81-5
Czech (1119) 84 Illustrated 120
Czechoslovakia (1124) 84 Illustrated 120

131

D

D & B Bottom (344) 11 Illustrated 38
Daisy & Bluebell 78
Daisy Trio (1149) 85 Illustrated 123
Daisy and Button (3, 61, 371, 376, 958, 974) 1, 2, 13, 78
　Illustrated 17, 20, 40, 107, 109
Dalzell, Gilmore & Leighton Co. 9
Dandelion (266) v, 9 Illustrated Front Cover, 33
Darwin (336) 11 Illustrated 38
Daum Nancy (157, 162, 164, 166, 168-9) 1, 5, 6 Illustrated 27
Dawn to Dusk Hat (365) 12 Illustrated 40
Deco Drape (984) 79 Illustrated 109
Dee Dee (1069) 82 Illustrated 116
Degenhart 81
Delft Diamond (1063) 82 Illustrated 115
Delinda (1127) 84 Illustrated 121
Derby Silver Co. 71-3, 75-7
Derby, The (270) 9 Illustrated 34
Dew Drops (1133) 84 Illustrated 121
Diamond Point (2) 1 Illustrated 17
Diamond Quilt (4, 9, 12, 20, 23-4, 26-7, 49, 52-3,
　79, 82, 86, 112, 119, 126, 136, 210, 212)
Diamond Quilt 1, 2, 3, 4, 5, 7 Illustrated 17, 18, 20, 22, 24-5, 30
Diamond Spearhead (277) 9 Illustrated 34
Diamond Waffle (257) 8 Illustrated 33
Diana (1011) 80 Illustrated 111
Dithridge & Co. 9, 10, 80
Divine (1132) 84 Illustrated 121
Dog with Hat (354) 12 Illustrated 39
Dolphins with Seashells (1027) 80 Illustrated 113
Dorflinger & Sons 82
Dorothy (1083) 82 Illustrated 117
Double Gourd (176) 6 Illustrated 28
Double Pinwheel (261) 8 Illustrated 33
Dover (1106) 83 Illustrated 119
Dugan Glass 3, 8, 10
Duncan #28 (269) 9 Illustrated 34
Duncan (1084) 82 Illustrated 117
Duncan Glass vi, 1, 7-9, 12, 86

E

E.S. Germany (458) 15 Illustrated 45
Early Tapered Block Hat (987) 79 Illustrated 110
Egg (153-5) 5 Illustrated 26
Elbe (1169) 85 Illustrated 124
Elena (1156) 85 Illustrated 123
Erwin (1080) 82 Illustrated 117

F

Fairborn (1136) 84 Illustrated 121
Fairborn Swirl (393) 13 Illustrated 41
Fairyland Lustre (573, 576) 66 Illustrated 53
Fancy Cut (1023) 80 Illustrated 112
Fancy Diamonds (962) 78 Illustrated 108
Fancy Elephant (358) 12 Illustrated 39
Fenton Art Glass vi, 8, 11-3, 86
Fern with Lily of the Valley (1013) 80 Illustrated 112
Fig Mold (35, 37, 39) 2 Illustrated 19
Findlay Flint Glass 78
Fine Rib (32-3) 1, 2 Illustrated 19
Five Cent Pail (347) 11 Illustrated 38
Flared Panels (1004) 80 Illustrated 111
Flared Round Panels (1029) 81 Illustrated 113
Flat to Round Panel (262) 8 Illustrated 33
Fleur de Lis (355) 12 Illustrated 39
Fleur de Lis and Fern (1035) 81 Illustrated 113
Florette (64, 978) 2, 79 Illustrated 21, 109
Florida (242) 81 Illustrated 32
Florist (1100) 83 Illustrated 118

Flower Delight (313) 10 Illustrated 36
Flower Form (13, 54) 1, 2 Illustrated 17, 20
Flute (956, 1008) 78, 80 Illustrated 111, 107
Foliage (1079) 82 Illustrated 117
Footed Ball (306) 10 Illustrated 36
Footed Devil (286) 9 Illustrated 35
Forbes Silver Co. 1, 76
Fostoria Glass Co. v, 9, 61, 77-9
Four Corners (1046) 81 Illustrated 114
Fractured Foil (57) 2 Illustrated 20
Framed Loop (284) 9 Illustrated 35
Free Form Three Lobe (342) 11 Illustrated 38
French Panels (287, 1017) 10, 80 Illustrated 35, 112
French Swirls (1018) 80 Illustrated 112
Frog Toothpick (333, 335) 11 Illustrated 38
Frosted Shells (1001) 80 Illustrated 111

G

Galle (161, 163, 167, 170) 5, 6 Illustrated 27
Galloway (385) 13 Illustrated 41
Genesis (1134) 84 Illustrated 121
Geneva (273) 9 Illustrated 34
Gillinder & Sons 81
Ginger (1161) 85 Illustrated 124
Glacier (1107) 83 Illustrated 119
Golden Waves (392) 13 Illustrated 41
Goppy (1078) 82 Illustrated 117
Gorham & Co. 74
Goss (508-11, 513-21, 523) xiv, 16, 65 Illustrated 49
Gravic Carnation (1057) 81 Illustrated 115
Grecian Column (295) 10 Illustrated 35
Green Opaque (206) 7 Illustrated 30
Greensburg Glass Co. 8
Guttate (75) 3 Illustrated 21

H

Hand Vase (332) 11 Illustrated 38
Hand with Fan (352) 12 Illustrated 39
Hartford Silver Plate Co. 77
Hawkes & Co. 81-2
Heart (292) 10 Illustrated 35
Heart in Sand (1024) 80 Illustrated 112
Heather (1101) 83 Illustrated 119
Heisey Co., A.H. v, 8, 9
Henry (1166) 85 Illustrated 124
Hexagonal Inverted Thumbprint (341) 11 Illustrated 38
High Handled Hexagon (945) 77 Illustrated 107
Hoare & Co. 81
Hobbs, Brockunier & Co. 3, 8, 78
Hobnail (314) 10 Illustrated 36
Holly Amber 78
Holly, Pedestalled (961) 78 Illustrated 108
Homan Manufacturing Co. 72, 76
Hooped Barrel Variant (294) 10 Illustrated 35
Hope (1065) 82 Illustrated 116
Hub (299) 10 Illustrated 35

I

Idyll (240, 280) 8, 9 Illustrated 32, 34
Illinois Gold (386) 13 Illustrated 41
Imperial Glass Co. 12, 78, 80
Indian Head Match (1025) 80 Illustrated 113
Indiana Glass Co. 8, 9, 78, 80
Indiana Tumbler & Goblet Co. 12, 78, 80
Indies (1128) 84 Illustrated 121
Ingrown Toes (1015) 80 Illustrated 112
Intaglio Vine and Flower (953) 78 Illustrated 107
Interlocked Hearts (963) 78 Illustrated 108
Inverted Thumbprint (7, 88, 94, 97, 99, 100, 107, 221, 230, 232, 343)
Inverted Thumbprint 1, 3, 4, 7, 11 Illustrated 17, 22-3, 31, 38

Iowa Belle (394) 14 Illustrated 41
Iowa City Glass 79
Iris (250) 8 Illustrated 32
Iris with Meander (250) 8 Illustrated 32
Ivy, Sandwich (1014) 80 Illustrated 112
J
Jasperware 66-7
Jefferson Glass Co. 7-9, 78
Jenkins Glass Co. 78-9
Jennings Brass Mfg. Co. 74
Jewel (1054) 81 Illustrated 115
Jo Ann (1047) 81 Illustrated 114
Judge (1059) 82 Illustrated 115
June (1111) 83 Illustrated 119
Juno (261) 8 Illustrated 33
K
Karma (1094) 83 Illustrated 118
Kemple 12, 79, 80
Kentucky (258) 8 Illustrated 33
Keystone (1036) 81 Illustrated 113
Kingfisher (985-6) 79 Illustrated 110
Knotty Pine (1034) 81 Illustrated 113
Kronheimer Oldenbusch Co. 75
L
Labino, Dominic 6
Lacy Floral (1022) 80 Illustrated 112
Ladders 80
Lafayette (1138) 84 Illustrated 122
Lancaster Glass Co. 79
Landwind (1095) 83 Illustrated 118
Late Westmoreland (238) 7 Illustrated 32
Laura (1098) 83 Illustrated 118
Leaf & Pleat (1026) 80 Illustrated 113
Leaf & Star (977) 79 Illustrated 109
Leaf Mold (76-7) vi, 3 Illustrated Back Cover, 21
Leaf Umbrella (67, 74) vi, 3 Illustrated Back Cover, 21
Leafy Scroll (1006) 80 Illustrated 111
Leah (1170) 85 Illustrated 124
Lee (1129) 84 Illustrated 121
Lenoir (1021) 80 Illustrated 112
Levi (1049) 81 Illustrated 114
Libbey 1, 3, 82-3, 85
Lilith (1102) 83 Illustrated 119
Lion Silver Co. 75
Locket on Chain (243) v, 8 Illustrated Front Cover, 32
Lockport (1074) 82 Illustrated 116
Loop-Footed (1034) 81 Illustrated 113
Lord Cork (1113) 83 Illustrated 120
Lotto (1068) 82 Illustrated 116
Lotton Art Glass 6, 7
Louisiana (994) 79 Illustrated 110
Lucy (1168) 85 Illustrated 124
Lundberg, James 6
M
Mabel (1053) 81 Illustrated 115
Madame Bovary (302) 10 Illustrated 36
Madolin(e) (259) 8 Illustrated 33
Majolica (473, 536, 636-8, 682) 16, 65, 68-9
   Illustrated 46, 50, 57, 60
Man with Pack on Back (350) 11 Illustrated 39
Manhattan Silverplate Co. 72, 76
Manila (965) 78 Illustrated 108
Mansfield (1081) 82 Illustrated 117
Maple City Glass Co. 81
Marble (1089) 83 Illustrated 118
Marco (1091) 83 Illustrated 118
Mary Gregory Type (98, 223) 4, 7 Illustrated 23, 31

Maypole (1130) 84 Illustrated 121
McBroom (1045) 81 Illustrated 114
McKee Colonial (980) 79 Illustrated 109
McKee Glass 8, 9, 11-2, 79, 81
McLain (1108) 83 Illustrated 119
Mebane (1162) 85 Illustrated 124
Mercury (1155) 85 Illustrated 123
Meriden Brittania Co. 73-4
Meriden Silverplate 1, 70-7
Mermod & Jaccard Jewelry Co. 72-4
Metal v, xii, xiii, 62-4, 70-7
Michael (1140) 84 Illustrated 122
Michigan (290) 10 Illustrated 35
Middle Silesia (1120) 84 Illustrated 120
Middletown Silver Co. 70-1, 74
Millard (260) 8 Illustrated 33
Millefiore (160, 373) 5, 13 Illustrated 27, 40
Mink (1056) 81 Illustrated 115
Model Flint Glass Co. 78
Monarch Silver Co. 76
Monet & Stumpf 2, 5
Monroe, C.F. 5, 81, 83
Moon Sign (1093) 83 Illustrated 118
Moravia (1123) 84 Illustrated 120
Moriage 16, 66
Moser 3, 7, 10-1
Mosser Glass 13
Mother of Pearl (49, 52-3, 112-4, 116, 118-9, 124) 2, 4
   Illustrated 20, 24
Mt. Washington 1-5, 7
N
NTHCS Commemoratives vi, 13-4, 86
Nakara (151-2) 5 Illustrated 26
National (247) 8 Illustrated 32
National Glass 3, 8-10
Nautilus 80
Nemesis (269) 9 Illustrated 34
Nestor (248) 8 Illustrated 32
Nevada (981) 79 Illustrated 109
New England Glass Co. v, 1, 3-5, 7
New Haven Silver Plate Co. 76
New Martinsville Glass Co. 79, 80
New Westmoreland (238) 7 Illustrated 32
Newgate (1097) 83 Illustrated 118
Nine Panel Colonial (955) 78 Illustrated 107
Nippon (460-70, 474, 476-83, 485-6, 488-91) xiv, 15-6
   Illustrated 46-7
No Bees (1033) 81 Illustrated 113
Noble (1152) 85 Illustrated 123
Noritake (471, 487) 15-6 Illustrated 46-7
Northwood Glass Co. vi, 2, 3, 7-10, 78-9, 86
Nouveau Art (383) 13 Illustrated 41
Nutmeg (1154) 85 Illustrated 123
O
Odd (1072) 82 Illustrated 116
Old Columbia (999) 79 Illustrated 111
Old Woman (361) 12 Illustrated 39
One-O-One (947) 77 Illustrated 107
Opaline (285, 288) 9, 10 Illustrated 35
Optic Tube (95) 3 Illustrated 23
Optic, Hobb's (66, 105) 3, 4 Illustrated 21, 23
Orinoco (968) 78 Illustrated 108
Orrefors Glass Co. 85
P
Page (1135) 84 Illustrated 121
Pagoda (1153) 85 Illustrated 123
Painted Post (387) 13 Illustrated 41

133

Pairpoint 1, 3, 12-3, 70-7
Pairpoint Butterfly (391) 13 Illustrated 41
Palm Leaf (297) 10 Illustrated 35
Pamona (130-2, 140) 5 Illustrated 25
Panama (988) 79 Illustrated 110
Panda (1151) 85 Illustrated 123
Panelled Daisy 13
Panelled Sprig (971) 78 Illustrated 108
Panelled Tulips (307) 10 Illustrated 36
Pansy (63) 2 Illustrated 21
Parallel Greek Key (211) 7 Illustrated 30
Parian Swirl (78) 3 Illustrated 21
Patron (1131) 84 Illustrated 121
Patton (1048) 81 Illustrated 114
Paula (1052) 81 Illustrated 114
Peachblow (15, 16, 111, 129, 133, 304, 369) 1, 4, 5, 10, 12 Illustrated 18, 24-5, 36, 40
Pedestalled Panel with Lens (998) 79 Illustrated 111
Peek-A-Boo (256, 353) 8, 12 Illustrated 33, 39
Peg Legs (1076) 82 Illustrated 116
Petalled Medallion (255) 8 Illustrated 33
Phoenix Glass Co. 4
Pilgrim (1103) 83 Illustrated 119
Pilgrim Glass Co. 7, 13
Pinstar (1104) 83 Illustrated 119
Pitkin and Brooks 82-3, 85
Placid (1000) 79 Illustrated 111
Placid Thumbprint 79
Plique-a-jour (229) 7 Illustrated 31
Pointed Gothic (972) 78 Illustrated 108
Pointed Panels with Ovals (337) 11 Illustrated 38
Polka Dot Hat (366) 12 Illustrated 40
Polly (1146) 85 Illustrated 122
Poole Silver Co. 71, 77
Pooter (1145, 1167) 85 Illustrated 122, 124
Portland (278) 9 Illustrated 34
Portland Glass 12
Pottery 68
Preparedness (1003) 80 Illustrated 111
Prima Donna (66, 105) 3, 4 Illustrated 21, 23
Priscilla (263) 9 Illustrated 33
Prismatic (1082) 82 Illustrated 117
Puritan (976) 79 Illustrated 109
Puritan, Tarentum's (1007) 80 Illustrated 111
Purple Martin (1171) 85 Illustrated 124

Q

Quaker City Cut Glass Co. 82
Quartz (1157) 85 Illustrated 123
Queen Mary (11, 53, 110) 1, 2, 4 Illustrated 17, 20, 24
Queen Victoria (304) 10 Illustrated 36
Quezal 6
Quilt (64, 978) 2, 79 Illustrated 21, 109
Quilted Phlox (68, 293) 3, 10 Illustrated 21, 35

R

R.S. Germany (444-6, 448-57, 459, 558) 15, 66 Illustrated 45, 52
R.S. Prussia (428-43, 564) xii, 15, 66 Illustrated 44, 52
R.S. Tillowitz (447) 15 Illustrated 45
Rabbit Match (253) 8 Illustrated 33
Rachel (1143) 84 Illustrated 122
Radium (1060) 82 Illustrated 115
Rainbow (312) 10 Illustrated 36
Raindrop Hat No. 1 (372) 12 Illustrated 40
Reed & Barton 72-3, 76
Rex (1023) 80 Illustrated 112
Ribbed Daisy Band (338) 11 Illustrated 38
Ribbed Drape (964) 78 Illustrated 108

Ribbed Opal Lattice (69) 3 Illustrated 21
Ribbed Thumbprint (282) 9 Illustrated 34
Rice's Sons, Bernard 77
Ring Base (108, 118, 241, 244) 4, 8 Illustrated 23-4, 32
Ring Neck Optic (66, 105) 3, 4 Illustrated 21, 23
Ringed Scoop (346) 11 Illustrated 38
Riverside #436 (255) 8 Illustrated 33
Riverside (270) 9 Illustrated 34
Riverside Glass 8, 9
Robin (1137) 84 Illustrated 122
Robinson Glass Co. 78-9
Rockford Silver Plate Co. 70-1, 74
Rogers Silver Co. 77
Rogers and Bros. 1, 72
Rogers, Smith & Co. 73-4
Royal Bayreuth (396-427) v, xiii, 14-5 Illustrated 42-3
Royal Bohemian (1114) 83 Illustrated 120
Royal Doulton (492-507, 512, 522) xiv, 16, 65 Illustrated 48-9
Royal Flemish (36, 39) 2 Illustrated 19
Royal Ivy (982, 1173) vi, 79, 86 Illustrated Back Cover, 109
Royal Silver 3
Rubina (90) 3 Illustrated 22

S

S-Repeat (247) 8 Illustrated 32
Sable (1055) 81 Illustrated 115
Sarah Tiffin (1144) 85 Illustrated 122
Saratoga (1058) 81 Illustrated 115
Scroll with Acanthus (245) 8 Illustrated 32
Scrolled Shell (1016) 80 Illustrated 112
Seaweed (251) 8 Illustrated 32
Servia (1116) 84 Illustrated 120
Sheffield 72
Shell & Scale (288) 10 Illustrated 35
Shell & Seaweed (275) 9 Illustrated 34
Shells & Flowers (1037) 81 Illustrated 113
Shellware (1030-1) 81 Illustrated 113
Shriner's Souvenir (106) 4 Illustrated 23
Shriner's Souvenir No. 2 (296) 10 Illustrated 35
Silesia (1122) 84 Illustrated 120
Silverplate v, xii, 70-7
Simple Scroll (38, 40-1) 2 Illustrated 19
Simpson, Hall & Miller 71-4
Six Panel Flare (345) 11 Illustrated 38
Skirted Optic (103) 4 Illustrated 23
Skookums (360) 12 Illustrated 39
Smith Bros. 5
Smith Glass 80
Snowflake (1086) 83 Illustrated 117
Southington C Company 70
Spatter Hat (375) 13 Illustrated 40
Spider (1090) 83 Illustrated 118
Spider Web (43, 46) 2 Illustrated 19
Spirit of '76 (380-2) 13 Illustrated 41
Squatty Bulb Variant (121) 4 Illustrated 24
St. Bernard (1062) 82 Illustrated 115
St. Clair Glass 79
St. Louie (1110) 83 Illustrated 119
St. Louis Glass 80
St. Louis Silver Co. 70
Star Feather (1064) 82 Illustrated 115
Star Whorl (261) 8 Illustrated 33
Stardust (1105) 83 Illustrated 119
Stars and Bars with Leaf (349) 11 Illustrated 39
Steuben Glass 6
Stevens Silver Co. 76
Stevens and Williams 4, 10
Stippled Forget-Me-Not (970) 78 Illustrated 108

Stockholm (1150) 85 Illustrated 123
Stove (359) 12 Illustrated 39
Studio (1009, 1012) 80 Illustrated 111
Stump (339) 11 Illustrated 38
Sugar Cane (1117) 84 Illustrated 120
Sultan (283) 9 Illustrated 34
Sumba (1042) 81 Illustrated 114
Sun Dance (1112) 83 Illustrated 119
Sun Dog (1070) 82 Illustrated 116
Sunbonnet Babies (396-8) 14 Illustrated 42
Sundew (1041) 81 Illustrated 114
Sunken Primrose (242) 8 Illustrated 32
Sunset (274) 9 Illustrated 34
Sunspot (1075) 82 Illustrated 116
Swag with Brackets (281) 9 Illustrated 34
Swallow (1043) 81 Illustrated 114
Swinger (259) 8 Illustrated 33
Swirl & Leaf (70) 3 Illustrated 21
Swirl & Rosette (300) 10 Illustrated 36
Swirl Mold (42, 44) 2 Illustrated 19
Swirled Tiny Fingers (36) 2 Illustrated 19

T

Tapered Block Hat (370) 12 Illustrated 40
Tapered Bulge (144) 5 Illustrated 26
Tapered Tiffin (1141-2) 84 Illustrated 122
Tapestry (400-3, 405-6, 408-11) v, 14 Illustrated Front Cover, v, 42
Tarentum Glass 80
Taylor Bros. 84
Tea Room (1002) 80 Illustrated 111
Tepee (269) 9 Illustrated 34
Terry (1163) 85 Illustrated 124
Texas Rose (384) 13 Illustrated 41
Thistle (1061) 82 Illustrated 115
Thistle Rose (1139) 84 Illustrated 122
Thor (1159) 85 Illustrated 123
Thorny Tree Trunk (96) 4 Illustrated 23
Threads of Gold (388) 13 Illustrated 41
Three Flowers (1040) 81 Illustrated 113
Three Fruits (969, 983) 78-9 Illustrated 108-9
Three In One (962) 78 Illustrated 108
Thumbnail (262) 8 Illustrated 33
Tiffany Glass 6
Tiffin Glass 84-5
Toboggan Shoe (348) 11 Illustrated 38
Tokyo (237, 276) 7, 9 Illustrated 32, 34
Tramp's Shoe (1038-9) 8 Illustrated 113
Tree of Life (357) 12 Illustrated 39
Tufts, James W. 1, 3, 70-4, 76
Twin Cities (1118) 84 Illustrated 120
Two Size Panel (954) 78 Illustrated 107

U

U.S. Diamond Block (257) 8 Illustrated 33
U.S. Flutes (990) 79 Illustrated 110
U.S. Glass Co. 8-13, 79, 80, 84
U.S.A. (254) 8 Illustrated 33
Umbrella Stand (301) 10 Illustrated 36
Uniontown (1158) 85 Illustrated 123
Upright Piano (362) 12 Illustrated 39

V

Val (1073) 82 Illustrated 116
Val (1164) 85 Illustrated 124
Van Burgh S.P. Co. 74, 77
Venecia (991) 79 Illustrated 110
Venetian Diamond (80-1, 84) 3 Illustrated 22
Victor Silver Co. (also see Derby) 75-6
Victoria, Fostoria's (948) 77 Illustrated 107
Vigilant (960) 78 Illustrated 107
Virginia (385) 13 Illustrated 41

W

Wallace Pewter 75
Wally (1126) 84 Illustrated 121
Water Flower (1109) 83 Illustrated 119
Waterford 83
Webb Corbett 82
Webb and Sons 1-5, 10
Weber (1077) 82 Illustrated 117
Webster, E.G. & Son 71, 76-7
Wedgwood 66
West Slavic (1115) 84 Illustrated 120
West Virginia Glass Co. 79
Westcott Silver Co. 73
Westmore land (238) 7 Illustrated 32
Westmoreland Glass Co. 7, 77, 80
Weston (967-8) 78 Illustrated 108
Wide Swirl (104, 249) 4, 8 Illustrated 23, 32
Wilcox Silver Plate Co. 70-1, 73, 75-6
Wild Rose with Scrolling (283) 9 Illustrated 34
Winged Scroll (272) 9 Illustrated 34
Winsome 80
Wishbone (963) 78 Illustrated 108
Witch Head (361) 12 Illustrated 39
Wm. Rogers Mfg. 1, 3, 71, 73, 75
Woodman-Cook Co. 75
Wreath & Shell (965) 78 Illustrated 108

Y

Yutec (992) 79 Illustrated 110

Z

Zanesville (995-6) 79 Illustrated 110
Zipper Edge Panels (265) 9 Illustrated 33
Zipper Slash (224, 226) 7 Illustrated 31
Zippered Corner (93) 3 Illustrated 23

Errata
(refer to item numbers)

41.   Ref: H-1000 #59 and 91.
283. Delete Refs to H-1000 #105 and 284.
292. Also made in blue. Ref: H-1 #141-142.
965. Should read "circa 1898."
1027. Delete (NBW); see Mighell, Plate XXX.

TOOTHPICK HOLDERS: CHINA, GLASS AND METAL

prepared by Members of the National Toothpick Holder Collectors Society

1993-94 Value Guide

Because so many of the toothpick holders are shown here for the first time, it was difficult to prepare this value guide. The market has yet to be established (or even "tested"), so some values reflect prices paid as well as the best judgments of experienced toothpick holder collectors.

"Collectibility" and "condition" affect the prices that collectors will pay. Some types of art glass, such as Burmese, have long been high-priced in response to collector demand, while other glass toothpick holders remain undiscovered and, hence, modestly priced. The demand for china and metal toothpick holders is on the increase, and this book should prove stimulating to those who seek them. Some items have been designated scarce (S), rare (R) or very rare (VR).

Values are for "mint" condition and, when applicable, original decoration; evidence of repair or chips/cracks have a strong impact on prices for glass and china toothpick holders, and those who collect metal toothpick holders are mindful of restorations as well as the characteristics of patina.

The NTHCS would like to express its appreciation to the following for their help with this value guide: Leighton A. Fossey; Bob McNamara; Bob Davis; and Russ Musgrove.

Neither the authors nor the publisher can be liable for losses incurred when using this guide as the basis for any transaction.

Fig.		Fig.		Fig.		Fig.		Fig.	
1 -	$ 275	38 -	750	75 -	150	112 -	400	149 -	150
2 -	150	39 -	1200 (VR)	76 -	175	113 -	100	150 -	150
3 -	135	40 -	160	77 -	175	114 -	100	151 -	75
4 -	500	41 -	200	78 -	125	115 -	150	152 -	350
5 -	120	42 -	200	79 -	300	116 -	100	153 -	80
6 -	500	43 -	275	80 -	450	117 -	350	154 -	80
7 -	200	44 -	200	81 -	425	118 -	200	155 -	80
8 -	500	45 -	275	82 -	300	119 -	150	156 -	175
9 -	500	46 -	275	83 -	1000	120 -	200	157 -	375
10 -	475	47 -	250	84 -	300	121 -	80	158 -	300
11 -	350	48 -	250	85 -	300	122 -	75	159 -	275
12 -	300	49 -	300	86 -	375	123 -	100	160 -	75
13 -	150	50 -	250	87 -	75	124 -	75	161 -	475
14 -	100	51 -	175	88 -	125	125 -	75	162 -	350
15 -	3000	52 -	400	89 -	75	126 -	50	163 -	400
16 -	3250	53 -	400	90 -	125	127 -	50	164 -	375
17 -	550	54 -	150	91 -	75	128 -	120	165 -	100
18 -	550	55 -	200	92 -	75	129 -	350	166 -	350
19 -	350	56 -	125	93 -	100	130 -	200	167 -	450
20 -	400	57 -	150	94 -	300	131 -	200	168 -	375
21 -	275	58 -	150	95 -	150	132 -	200	169 -	375
22 -	500	59 -	175	96 -	75	133 -	100	170 -	475
23 -	450	60 -	100	97 -	60	134 -	100	171 -	300
24 -	450	61 -	50	98 -	50	135 -	75	172 -	175
25 -	450	62 -	50	99 -	140	136 -	50	173 -	150
26 -	450	63 -	60	100 -	100	137 -	60	174 -	350
27 -	450	64 -	125	101 -	75	138 -	700	175 -	250
28 -	275	65 -	75	102 -	100	139 -	50	176 -	350
29 -	450	66 -	200	103 -	125	140 -	250	177 -	250
30 -	650 (VR)	67 -	225	104 -	100	141 -	40	178 -	350
31 -	145	68 -	150	105 -	200	142 -	150	179 -	375
32 -	275	69 -	250	106 -	250	143 -	275	180 -	275
33 -	300	70 -	200	107 -	100	144 -	95 (R)	181 -	300
34 -	100	71 -	150 (S)	108 -	150	145 -	80	182 -	300
35 -	500	72 -	225	109 -	300	146 -	750	183 -	300
36 -	750 (VR)	73 -	150	110 -	275	147 -	600	184 -	200
37 -	1500 (VR)	74 -	175	111 -	225	148 -	35	185 -	300

Fig.			Fig.			Fig.			Fig.			Fig.		
186 -	300		255 -	95		324 -	30		393 -	25		462 -	40	
187 -	275		256 -	60		325 -	40		394 -	25		463 -	50	
188 -	200		257 -	80		326 -	40		395 -	35		464 -	45	
189 -	40		258 -	150		327 -	40		396 -	425		465 -	40	
190 -	40		259 -	45		328 -	30		397 -	425		466 -	40	
191 -	40		260 -	150	(S)	329 -	30		398 -	425		467 -	45	
192 -	40		261 -	75		330 -	45		399 -	125		468 -	40	
193 -	40		262 -	120	(S)	331 -	50		400 -	400		469 -	40	
194 -	40		263 -	75		332 -	30		401 -	325		470 -	35	
195 -	35		264 -	75	(S)	333 -	80		402 -	425		471 -	40	
196 -	40		265 -	75		334 -	100		403 -	350		472 -	40	
197 -	40		266 -	100	(S)	335 -	80		404 -	125		473 -	45	
198 -	40		267 -	55		336 -	85		405 -	500		474 -	35	
199 -	35		268 -	60		337 -	50		406 -	325		475 -	25	
200 -	35		269 -	70		338 -	40		407 -	95		476 -	45	
201 -	40		270 -	75	(S)	339 -	50		408 -	325		477 -	50	
202 -	40		271 -	60		340 -	75		409 -	450		478 -	50	
203 -	40		272 -	130		341 -	190		410 -	400		479 -	50	
204 -	40		273 -	160	(S)	342 -	75		411 -	400		480 -	50	
205 -	1000	(VR)	274 -	55		343 -	75		412 -	135		481 -	45	
206 -	750		275 -	90	(S)	344 -	45		413 -	135		482 -	40	
207 -	500		276 -	200	(S)	345 -	25		414 -	150		483 -	45	
208 -	700		277 -	90		346 -	25		415 -	135		484 -	45	
209 -	125		278 -	75	(S)	347 -	25		416 -	135		485 -	40	
210 -	250		279 -	100	(R)	348 -	50		417 -	150		486 -	45	
211 -	300		280 -	90		349 -	75		418 -	225		487 -	40	
212 -	450		281 -	200	(S)	350 -	50		419 -	135		488 -	50	
213 -	25		282 -	50		351 -	50		420 -	180		489 -	45	
214 -	30		283 -	50		352 -	45		421 -	210		490 -	45	
215 -	25		284 -	40		353 -	45		422 -	95		491 -	50	
216 -	25		285 -	50		354 -	70		423 -	195		492 -	85	
217 -	25		286 -	50		355 -	70		424 -	135		493 -	85	
218 -	25		287 -	50		356 -	40		425 -	170		494 -	85	
219 -	25		288 -	40		357 -	30		426 -	195		495 -	85	
220 -	25		289 -	40		358 -	50		427 -	195		496 -	90	
221 -	35		290 -	75		359 -	25		428 -	395	(R)	497 -	85	
222 -	35		291 -	50		360 -	25		429 -	375		498 -	75	
223 -	35		292 -	50		361 -	35		430 -	395	(R)	499 -	75	
224 -	75		293 -	125	(S)	362 -	25		431 -	175		500 -	75	
225 -	60		294 -	45		363 -	25		432 -	275		501 -	75	
226 -	75		295 -	50		364 -	25		433 -	280	(S)	502 -	85	
227 -	30		296 -	175		365 -	30		434 -	250		503 -	75	
228 -	40		297 -	50		366 -	30		435 -	350	(R)	504 -	85	
229 -	40		298 -	40		367 -	30		436 -	325		505 -	75	
230 -	45		299 -	40		368 -	25		437 -	395	(VR)	506 -	85	
231 -	35		300 -	35		369 -	65		438 -	325	(S)	507 -	85	
232 -	75		301 -	45		370 -	30		439 -	225		508 -	40	
233 -	45		302 -	30		371 -	30		440 -	225		509 -	35	
234 -	50		303 -	40		372 -	40		441 -	175		510 -	35	
235 -	35		304 -	350	(S)	373 -	20		442 -	185		511 -	40	
236 -	35		305 -	45		374 -	25		443 -	300	(S)	512 -	75	
237 -	150		306 -	40		375 -	30		444 -	125		513 -	30	
238 -	75		307 -	50		376 -	25		445 -	125		514 -	35	
239 -	175		308 -	50		377 -	30		446 -	90		515 -	40	
240 -	300	(R)	309 -	50		378 -	25		447 -	100		516 -	40	
241 -	90		310 -	45		379 -	25		448 -	225		517 -	40	
242 -	250	(R)	311 -	50		380 -	10		449 -	175		518 -	35	
243 -	900	(VR)	312 -	40		381 -	10		450 -	200		519 -	40	
244 -	90		313 -	35		382 -	12		451 -	200		520 -	40	
245 -	150	(S)	314 -	35		383 -	10		452 -	175		521 -	35	
246 -	75		315 -	35		384 -	75		453 -	100		522 -	50	
247 -	50		316 -	35		385 -	20		454 -	100		523 -	35	
248 -	60		317 -	35		386 -	15		455 -	125		524 -	25	
249 -	45		318 -	30		387 -	10		456 -	100		525 -	30	
250 -	75		319 -	35		388 -	15		457 -	100		526 -	30	
251 -	60		320 -	35		389 -	15		458 -	90		527 -	30	
252 -	100		321 -	45		390 -	15		459 -	100		528 -	50	
253 -	65		322 -	45		391 -	25		460 -	45		529 -	45	
254 -	50		323 -	30		392 -	30		461 -	35		530 -	45	

Fig.		Fig.		Fig.		Fig.		Fig.		
531 -	45	600 -	65	669 -	35	738 -	75	807 -	65	
532 -	40	601 -	25	670 -	40	739 -	110	808 -	70	
533 -	30	602 -	35	671 -	40	740 -	95	809 -	70	
534 -	50	603 -	25	672 -	45	741 -	95	810 -	60	
535 -	50	604 -	25	673 -	35	742 -	95	811 -	65	
536 -	45	605 -	45	674 -	40	743 -	80	812 -	75	
537 -	50	606 -	40	675 -	35	744 -	85	813 -	80	
538 -	50	607 -	45	676 -	30	745 -	90	814 -	95	
539 -	50	608 -	45	677 -	40	746 -	90	815 -	90	
540 -	25	609 -	50	678 -	45	747 -	75	816 -	70	
541 -	50	610 -	45	679 -	40	748 -	50	817 -	70	
542 -	35	611 -	40	680 -	50	749 -	75	818 -	55	
543 -	30	612 -	45	681 -	45	750 -	85	819 -	75	(R)
544 -	45	613 -	50	682 -	40	751 -	75	820 -	65	
545 -	25	614 -	50	683 -	30	752 -	95	821 -	60	
546 -	30	615 -	45	684 -	50	753 -	75	822 -	60	
547 -	35	616 -	45	685 -	45	754 -	85	823 -	60	
548 -	50	617 -	45	686 -	40	755 -	80	824 -	65	
549 -	25	618 -	40	687 -	30	756 -	90	825 -	60	
550 -	30	619 -	55	688 -	35	757 -	50	826 -	60	
551 -	40	620 -	20	689 -	50	758 -	60	827 -	65	
552 -	50	621 -	20	690 -	50	759 -	50	828 -	55	
553 -	50	622 -	25	691 -	25	760 -	150	(R)	829 -	60	
554 -	25	623 -	25	692 -	30	761 -	175	(R)	830 -	65	
555 -	50	624 -	25	693 -	25	762 -	150	(R)	831 -	75	
556 -	50	625 -	25	694 -	40	763 -	100	832 -	75	
557 -	40	626 -	30	695 -	50	764 -	50	833 -	60	
558 -	100	627 -	25	696 -	50	765 -	100	834 -	60	
559 -	45	628 -	25	697 -	40	766 -	85	835 -	50	
560 -	40	629 -	30	698 -	125	767 -	90	836 -	100	
561 -	50	630 -	25	699 -	150	768 -	50	837 -	95	
562 -	50	631 -	30	700 -	125	769 -	45	838 -	75	
563 -	40	632 -	45	701 -	125	770 -	75	839 -	85	
564 -	125	633 -	25	702 -	75	771 -	60	840 -	60	
565 -	50	634 -	40	703 -	75	772 -	60	841 -	60	
566 -	150	635 -	50	704 -	75	773 -	50	842 -	60	
567 -	50	636 -	50	705 -	90	774 -	60	843 -	60	
568 -	30	637 -	50	706 -	100	775 -	70	844 -	90	
569 -	50	638 -	50	707 -	50	776 -	45	845 -	80	
570 -	40	639 -	55	708 -	75	777 -	100	846 -	55	
571 -	100	640 -	40	709 -	125	778 -	75	847 -	90	
572 -	45	641 -	45	710 -	125	779 -	80	848 -	65	
573 -	175	642 -	50	711 -	90	780 -	95	849 -	65	
574 -	65	643 -	40	712 -	75	781 -	100	850 -	50	
575 -	60	644 -	60	713 -	50	782 -	70	Needs holder		
576 -	175	645 -	45	714 -	125	783 -	90	851 -	50	
577 -	175	646 -	40	715 -	130	784 -	65	852 -	60	
578 -	95	647 -	30	716 -	120	785 -	90	853 -	50	
579 -	125	648 -	30	717 -	140	786 -	90	854 -	70	
580 -	90	649 -	35	718 -	90	787 -	100	855 -	65	
581 -	95	650 -	30	719 -	95	788 -	75	856 -	50	
582 -	75	651 -	50	720 -	75	789 -	50	857 -	50	
583 -	75	652 -	35	721 -	75	790 -	60	858 -	55	
584 -	125	653 -	35	722 -	100	791 -	40	859 -	65	
585 -	50	654 -	35	723 -	75	792 -	65	860 -	70	
586 -	50	655 -	50	724 -	70	793 -	75	861 -	50	
587 -	60	656 -	35	725 -	115	794 -	70	862 -	55	
588 -	60	657 -	40	726 -	100	795 -	70	863 -	60	
589 -	45	658 -	45	727 -	115	796 -	85	864 -	75	
590 -	50	659 -	35	728 -	95	797 -	90	865 -	65	
591 -	40	660 -	30	729 -	100	798 -	70	866 -	65	
592 -	50	661 -	45	730 -	90	799 -	90	867 -	45	
593 -	50	662 -	30	731 -	150	800 -	95	868 -	50	
594 -	45	663 -	45	732 -	95	801 -	90	869 -	65	
595 -	40	664 -	45	733 -	90	802 -	85	870 -	75	
596 -	50	665 -	45	734 -	130	803 -	100	871 -	45	
597 -	65	666 -	40	735 -	90	804 -	75	872 -	60	
598 -	65	667 -	45	736 -	85	805 -	65	873 -	55	
599 -	65	668 -	40	737 -	80	806 -	70	874 -	75	

Fig.		Fig.		Fig.		Fig.		Fig.	
875 -	70	944 -	30	1013 -	20	1082 -	30	1151 -	50
876 -	60	945 -	65	1014 -	25	1083 -	55	1152 -	45
877 -	60	946 -	60	1015 -	25	1084 -	55	1153 -	100
878 -	65	947 -	125	1016 -	25	1085 -	45	1154 -	40
879 -	75	948 -	175	1017 -	25	1086 -	60	1155 -	35
880 -	60	949 -	75	1018 -	30	1087 -	75	1156 -	35
881 -	60	950 -	50	1019 -	25	1088 -	65	1157 -	30
882 -	50	951 -	50	1020 -	20	1089 -	60	1158 -	55
883 -	45	952 -	50	1021 -	30	1090 -	45	1159 -	30
884 -	75	953 -	50	1022 -	35	1091 -	90	1160 -	50
885 -	65	954 -	60	1023 -	45	1092 -	40	1161 -	135
886 -	65	955 -	50	1024 -	75 (R)	1093 -	45	1162 -	65
887 -	60	956 -	60	1025 -	35	1094 -	85	1163 -	75
888 -	50	957 -	50	1026 -	50	1095 -	45	1164 -	100
889 -	50	958 -	50	1027 -	25	1096 -	75	1165 -	60
890 -	60	959 -	40	1028 -	25	1097 -	45	1166 -	65
891 -	60	960 -	75	1029 -	20	1098 -	40	1167 -	45
892 -	50	961 -	2500	1030 -	25	1099 -	55	1168 -	80
893 -	55	962 -	30	1031 -	25	1100 -	45	1169 -	55
894 -	60	963 -	30	1032 -	25	1101 -	40	1170 -	80
895 -	55	964 -	25	1033 -	20	1102 -	75	1171 -	100
896 -	70	965 -	45	1034 -	25	1103 -	50	1172 -	55
897 -	65	966 -	45	1035 -	30	1104 -	50	1173 -	65
898 -	65	967 -	45	1036 -	45	1105 -	45	1174 -	25
899 -	70	968 -	40	1037 -	25	1106 -	30		
900 -	60	969 -	40	1038 -	25	1107 -	50		
901 -	65	970 -	50	1039 -	25	1108 -	35		
902 -	70	971 -	50	1040 -	20	1109 -	45		
903 -	65	972 -	35	1041 -	75	1110 -	50		
904 -	65	973 -	50	1042 -	50	1111 -	35		
905 -	60	974 -	40	1043 -	45	1112 -	45		
906 -	55	975 -	35	1044 -	85	1113 -	55		
907 -	60	976 -	45	1045 -	55	1114 -	35		
908 -	60	977 -	50	1046 -	40	1115 -	30		
909 -	60	978 -	50	1047 -	45	1116 -	35		
910 -	50	979 -	45	1048 -	120	1117 -	55		
911 -	50	980 -	45	1049 -	100	1118 -	55		
912 -	45	981 -	60	1050 -	110	1119 -	30		
913 -	75	982 -	75	1051 -	55	1120 -	30		
914 -	65	983 -	40	1052 -	60	1121 -	40		
915 -	65	984 -	50	1053 -	120	1122 -	30		
916 -	60	985 -	30	1054 -	180	1123 -	35		
917 -	55	986 -	20	1055 -	85	1124 -	35		
918 -	70	987 -	45	1056 -	125	1125 -	60		
919 -	75	988 -	40	1057 -	210	1126 -	50		
920 -	65	989 -	60 (S)	1058 -	125	1127 -	65		
921 -	60	990 -	35	1059 -	195	1128 -	45		
922 -	65	991 -	50	1060 -	125	1129 -	45		
923 -	70	992 -	40	1061 -	125	1130 -	45		
924 -	65	993 -	40	1062 -	130	1131 -	55		
925 -	65	994 -	45	1063 -	25	1132 -	50		
926 -	60	995 -	45	1064 -	115	1133 -	65		
927 -	60	996 -	45	1065 -	95	1134 -	40		
928 -	60	997 -	30	1066 -	45	1135 -	45		
929 -	60	998 -	35	1067 -	45	1136 -	50		
930 -	55	999 -	45	1068 -	125	1137 -	95		
931 -	60	1000 -	40	1069 -	40	1138 -	55		
932 -	40	1001 -	30	1070 -	60	1139 -	40		
933 -	35	1002 -	20	1071 -	85	1140 -	45		
934 -	40	1003 -	195 (VR)	1072 -	130	1141 -	50		
935 -	35	1004 -	35	1073 -	100	1142 -	30		
936 -	40	1005 -	25	1074 -	85	1143 -	65		
937 -	35	1006 -	30	1075 -	60	1144 -	45		
938 -	35	1007 -	30	1076 -	225	1145 -	45		
939 -	35	1008 -	25	1077 -	45	1146 -	65		
940 -	40	1009 -	30	1078 -	85	1147 -	40		
941 -	35	1010 -	30	1079 -	75	1148 -	45		
942 -	35	1011 -	30	1080 -	95	1149 -	45		
943 -	40	1012 -	30	1081 -	40	1150 -	65		